Target
Get back on track 5

AQA GCSE (9–1)
German
Writing

Paul Shannon

Published by Pearson Education Limited, 80 Strand, London, WC2R ORL.

www.pearsonschoolsandfecolleges.co.uk

Text © Pearson Education Limited 2017
Produced by Out of House Publishing
Typeset by Newgen KnowledgeWorks Pvt. Ltd., Chennai, India

The right of Paul Shannon to be identified as author of this work has been asserted by him in accordance with the Copyright, Designs and Patents Act 1988.

First published 2017

20 19 18 17
10 9 8 7 6 5 4 3 2 1

British Library Cataloguing in Publication Data
A catalogue record for this book is available from the British Library

ISBN 978 0435 18913 6

Printed in Italy by Lego

Picture Credits
The publisher would like to thank the following individuals and organisations for permission to reproduce photographs:

(Key: b-bottom; c-centre; l-left; r-right; t-top)

123RF: Cathy Yeulet, 1; Cathy Yeulet, 2; Jasmin Merdan, 3; Stockbroker, 4; **Shutterstock:** oliveromg, 7; oliveromg, 8

All other images © Pearson Education

Note from the publisher
Pearson has robust editorial processes, including answer and fact checks, to ensure the accuracy of the content in this publication, and every effort is made to ensure this publication is free of errors. We are, however, only human, and occasionally errors do occur. Pearson is not liable for any misunderstandings that arise as a result of errors in this publication, but it is our priority to ensure that the content is accurate. If you spot an error, please do contact us at resourcescorrections@pearson.com so we can make sure it is corrected.

 This workbook has been developed using the Pearson Progression Map and Scale for German.

To find out more about the Progression Scale for German and to see how it relates to indicative GCSE 9–1 grades go to www.pearsonschools.co.uk/ProgressionServices

Helping you to formulate grade predictions, apply interventions and track progress.

Any reference to indicative grades in the Pearson Target Workbooks and Pearson Progression Services is not to be used as an accurate indicator of how a student will be awarded a grade for their GCSE exams.

You have told us that mapping the Steps from the Pearson Progression Maps to indicative grades will make it simpler for you to accumulate the evidence to formulate your own grade predictions, apply any interventions and track student progress. We're really excited about this work and its potential for helping teachers and students. It is, however, important to understand that this mapping is for guidance only to support teachers' own predictions of progress and is not an accurate predictor of grades.

Our Pearson Progression Scale is criterion referenced. If a student can perform a task or demonstrate a skill, we say they are working at a certain Step according to the criteria. Teachers can mark assessments and issue results with reference to these criteria which do not depend on the wider cohort in any given year. For GCSE exams however, all Awarding Organisations set the grade boundaries with reference to the strength of the cohort in any given year. For more information about how this works please visit: https://www.gov.uk/government/news/setting-standards-for-new-gcses-in-2017

Contents

1 Adding interest and clarity to your writing

Get started	1
1 How do I add interest to my descriptions?	3
2 How do I make my descriptions more engaging?	4
3 How do I write more accurately?	5
Sample response	6
Your turn!	7
Review your skills	8

2 Making your meaning clear

Get started	9
1 How do I write clear sentences in German?	11
2 How do I avoid being over-ambitious?	12
3 How do I write logically?	13
Sample response	14
Your turn!	15
Review your skills	16

3 Improving your accuracy

Get started	17
1 How do I improve the accuracy of my verb and case endings?	19
2 How do I improve the accuracy of my word order?	20
3 How do I improve my spelling?	21
Sample response	22
Your turn!	23
Review your skills	24

4 Writing effectively about the past

Get started	25
1 How do I use opportunities to write about the past?	27
2 How do I vary my references to the past to add interest?	28
3 How do I ensure that my past tense verbs are correct?	29
Sample response	30
Your turn!	31
Review your skills	32

5 Writing effectively about the future

Get started	33
1 How do I use opportunities to write about the future?	35
2 How do I vary my references to the future to add interest?	36
3 How do I ensure that my verbs referring to the future are correct?	37
Sample response	38
Your turn!	39
Review your skills	40

6 Choosing and linking your ideas

Get started	41
1 How do I choose appropriate material using language that I know?	43
2 How do I organise my writing?	44
3 How do I use conjunctions appropriately?	45
Sample response	46
Your turn!	47
Review your skills	48

7 Giving and explaining your opinions

Get started	49
1 How do I make my opinions relevant to the topic?	51
2 How do I add detail to my opinions?	52
3 How do I justify my opinions?	53
Sample response	54
Your turn!	55
Review your skills	56

8 Translating from English into German

Get started	57
1 How do I avoid translating too literally?	59
2 How do I translate precisely without paraphrasing?	60
3 How do I avoid the pitfalls of translation?	61
Sample response	62
Your turn!	63
Review your skills	64

9 Using complex language effectively

Get started	65
1 How do I broaden my range of vocabulary?	67
2 How do I broaden my range of grammatical structures?	68
3 How do I use idiom effectively?	69
Sample response	70
Your turn!	71
Review your skills	72

Answers   73

① Adding interest and clarity to your writing

This unit will help you learn how to add interest and clarity to your writing. The skills you will build are to:

- add interest to your descriptions
- make your descriptions more engaging
- write more accurately.

In the exam, you will be asked to tackle short writing tasks like the ones below. This unit will prepare you to plan and write your own responses to these questions.

Exam-style question

Du schickst dieses Foto von deiner Schule an deine Freundin in der Schweiz.

Schreib **vier** Sätze auf **Deutsch** über das Foto.

(8 marks)

Exam-style question

Du schreibst an deinen deutschen Freund über deine Schule.

Schreib etwas über:

- dein Lieblingsfach
- die anderen Schulfächer
- den Schultag
- die Schulordnung.

Du musst ungefähr **40** Wörter auf **Deutsch** schreiben.

(16 marks)

The three key questions in the **skills boosts** will help you add interest and clarity to your writing.

 1 How do I add interest to my descriptions?

 2 How do I make my descriptions more engaging?

 3 How do I write more accurately?

Look at the sample student responses to these questions on the next page.

Exam-style question

Du schickst dieses Foto von deiner Schule an deine Freundin in der Schweiz.

Schreib **vier** Sätze auf **Deutsch** über das Foto.

(8 marks)

1 _Wir sind in einem Klassenzimmer in einer britischen Schule._

2 _Es gibt sechs Schülerinnen und Schüler und eine Lehrerin mit langen Haaren._

3 _Die Schülerinnen und Schüler finden die Stunde interessant._

4 _Die Lehrerin stellt eine Frage._

(1) Read these statements and tick ✓ the three things that are mentioned in the student's answer above.

a We're in a British school. ☐

b The students are wearing uniform. ☐

c The students are asking questions. ☐

d There are female and male students. ☐

e The teacher has long hair. ☐

f The classroom has a notice board. ☐

Exam-style question

Du schreibst an deinen deutschen Freund über deine Schule.

Schreib etwas über:

- dein Lieblingsfach
- die anderen Schulfächer
- den Schultag
- die Schulordnung.

Du musst ungefähr **40** Wörter auf **Deutsch** schreiben. (16 marks)

Die Schule beginnt um 08:45 Uhr ☐ B3 _. Wir haben sechs Stunden pro Tag_ ☐ _. Mein Lieblingsfach ist Mathe_ ☐ _. Es ist einfach und ich bekomme gute Noten_ ☐ _. Geschichte und Erdkunde mache ich nicht gern_ ☐ _. Im Klassenzimmer dürfen wir nicht essen und trinken_ ☐ _. Wir müssen pünktlich sein_ ☐ _._

(2) Read the student's response above. Label ✎ the sentences B1–B4 to show which bullet point in the question they relate to.

(3) Which of these sentences could be included in an answer to the exam-style question above? Label ✎ the sentences NR if they are not relevant or B1–B4 to show which bullet point they relate to.

a Meine Schule ist ziemlich klein. ☐

b Die Schule endet um halb vier. ☐

c Wir dürfen nicht rauchen. ☐

d Biologie ist sehr schwierig. ☐

e Wir müssen in der Bibliothek ruhig sein. ☐

f In den Sommerferien fahren wir nach London. ☐

g Jede Stunde dauert fünfundfünfzig Minuten. ☐

h Ich mache am liebsten Chemie, denn es ist interessant. ☐

1 How do I add interest to my descriptions?

When you write a description you can add interest by using precise and varied vocabulary.

1 Look again at the two exam-style questions on page 2. Think of three different adjectives to describe each of these aspects of school life. Write 🖊 them in the table.

Lehrer/Lehrerin	Fächer	Schülerinnen/ Schüler	Klassenzimmer	Schultag
intelligent	....	....	....	....
streng	....	....	....	....
lustig	....	....	....	....

2 Look at the photo below and complete 🖊 the sentences with the appropriate words from the box.

| groß | glücklich | klein | freundlich |

1 Das Klassenzimmer ist ....

2 Die Schülerinnen und Schüler sind ....

3 Der Lehrer ist ....

4 Die Tafel ist ....

3 Use qualifiers to make your descriptions more precise and interesting. Complete 🖊 these sentences using a qualifier from the hint box and an adjective of your choice. Use all three qualifiers and as many different adjectives as you can.

zu	too
sehr	very
ziemlich	rather

a Meine Englischlehrerin ist ....sehr.. lustig................ .

b Die Schülerinnen und Schüler in meiner Klasse sind ....

c Die Schulordnung in meiner Schule ist ....

d Der Schultag ist ....

e Mein Klassenzimmer ist ....

f Deutsch ist ....

2 How do I make my descriptions more engaging?

You can improve your descriptions by:
- avoiding repetition
- using different verbs
- linking two or three pieces of information with *und* or *aber*
- using a variety of sentence openers.

1 a Read the student's description of this photo. It is rather plain and repetitive. Underline Ⓐ any words or phrases in the description that are repeated.

1 *Das ist eine Klasse.*

2 *Das ist ein Klassenzimmer.*

3 *Es gibt eine Lehrerin.*

4 *Es gibt Schülerinnen und Schüler.*

b Complete ✏️ this improved version of the answer, using the words and phrases in the box.

britischen	lernen	sehe	spricht	Stunde	ziemlich

1 *Das ist eine Klasse in einer .... Schule.*

2 *Das Klassenzimmer ist .... klein.*

3 *Ich .... eine Lehrerin und sie .... mit der Klasse.*

4 *Die Schülerinnen und Schüler .... Chemie und finden die*

.... interessant.

2 Practise beginning your sentences with different expressions to engage the reader.
Draw lines ✏️ to match each sentence beginning with the appropriate sentence ending.

A Ich sehe
B Auf dem Foto
C Es gibt
D Meiner Meinung nach

a sind neun Personen.
b ein Klassenzimmer.
c vier Schülerinnen und vier Schüler.
d sind wir in einem gemischten Gymnasium.

You can use these sentence openers to make your description of any topic or photo more interesting and less repetitive.

3 Now write ✏️ on paper a short description of the photo of the teacher and pupils on page 3. Make it engaging by using some of the techniques you have learned on this page.

3 **How do I write more accurately?**

Errors can obstruct or even prevent communication, so try to write as accurately as possible. Things to watch out for in German include:

- verbs: must agree with the subject (for example, *ich finde, er/sie/es findet, sie finden,* etc.)
- nouns: correct singular or plural form; gender; capital letter
- correct word order
- common spelling patterns such as umlaut, *sch, ei/ie*.

1 a Look at these words and phrases. Tick ✓ the box if the German is correct and cross ✗ the box if it is incorrect. Use the bullets points at the top of the page to help you.

i	die shule	
ii	ein Klassenzimmer	
iii	die Schulerinnen	
iv	interessant	
v	Der Lehrerin ist streng.	
vi	Ich nicht mag Mathe.	
vii	Wir essen in der Kantine.	
viii	Wir müssen sein pünktlich.	

b Circle Ⓐ the part of each word or phrase that is incorrect. Then write ✐ the correct version on the line.

2 All of these sentences contain errors. Circle Ⓐ the errors and write ✐ the correct word or phrase above them. You can check your answers by referring back to the correct version on page 2.

1 Wir ist in einem klassenzimmer in einer britischen shule.

2 Es gibt sechs Schulerinnen und Schuler und ein Lehrerin mit langen Haaren.

3 Der Schülerinnen und Schüler findet die Stunde interresant.

4 Die Lehrerin stellen eine Frage.

3 Read this response to the 40-word question on page 2. Circle Ⓐ the correct version of each word or phrase.

Mein **Leiblingsfach** / **Lieblingsfach** ist Kunst, denn die Stunden sind **interessant** / **interresant**. Ich **mag** / **Mag** Chemie nicht, denn **die** / **der** Lehrer **ist** / **sind** zu streng. **Der** / **Die** Schule beginnt um 9 Uhr und **endet um 4 Uhr** / **um 4 Uhr endet**. Wir **muss** / **müssen** eine Schuluniform tragen und **punktlich** / **pünktlich** sein. Man **darf** / **dürfen** nur in der Kantine **essen** / **isst**.

Sample response

Here is a 40-word writing task of the type you will answer in the exam. Read the two student answers. Neither is perfect, but which is better? Complete ① to help you decide.

Exam-style question

Du schreibst an deine Freundin in Österreich über deine Schule.

Schreib etwas über:

- deine Lehrerinnen und Lehrer
- was du in der Schule gut findest
- Hausaufgaben
- eine Klassenfahrt.

Du musst ungefähr **40** Wörter auf **Deutsch** schreiben.

(16 marks)

A

Ich habe viele Lehrerinnen und Lehrer. Sie sind freundlich, aber streng. Mein Leiblingsfach ist Musik, denn ich singe gern und die hausaufgaben sind einfach. Ich finde die Schulordnung gut. Wir dürfen nicht schlagen und mussen pünktlich sein. Nächste Woche werde wir fünf tage auf Klassenfahrt gehen.

B

Meine Lehrerinnen und Lehrer sind gut. Mein Lieblingsfach ist Musik. Musik ist gut. Die Hausaufgaben sind gut. Die Schulordnung ist gut. Wir dürfen nicht schlagen. Wir müssen pünktlich sein. Das ist auch gut. Wir gehen auf Klassenfahrt. Das ist gut.

① Complete the table by ticking ✓ column A or B and giving 🖉 an example.

Which answer...	A	B	How is this done? Note the German words used.
a avoids repeating common adjectives?	✓		*freundlich, einfach*
b uses a range of verbs?			
c joins related ideas using *und* and *aber*?			
d avoids errors with spelling, capital letters and verb endings?			

② On paper, use these student notes to write 🖉 a different 40-word response to the exam-style question above. Use the table in ① to help you.

Lehrerinnen und Lehrer nicht streng / Essen gut / Schulordnung nicht gut / zu viele Hausaufgaben / Klassenfahrt morgen

Your turn!

You are now going to plan your response to this exam-style task.

1 Plan your answer. Write ✏ some vocabulary in German in the table. Make sure you include a range of vocabulary (adjectives, nouns, verbs, qualifiers).

Bullet point	Vocabulary
die Klassenzimmer, Labors und so weiter	
deine Schulfächer	
Gruppen und Clubs	
was du in der Schule **nicht** magst	

Remember to revise useful school vocabulary such as school subjects and objects (table, chairs, etc).

2 Now write ✏ your response to the exam-style question.

Checklist	✓
In my answer do I ...	
include a range of adjectives and qualifiers?	
make my writing engaging by using a range of different verbs?	
link information with *und* and *aber* correctly?	
use a range of different sentence beginnings?	
ensure my verb endings, spellings, capital letters, genders and word order are correct?	

Review your skills

Check up

Review your response to the exam-style question on page 7. Tick ✓ the column to show how well you think you have done each of the following.

	Not quite ✓	Nearly there ✓	Got it! ✓
added interest to my descriptions	☐	☐	☐
made my descriptions more engaging	☐	☐	☐
written more accurately	☐	☐	☐

Need more practice?

On paper, plan and write 🖊 your response to the exam-style tasks below.

Exam-style question

Du schickst dieses Foto an deine Freundin in Österreich. Es zeigt die Schule von deinem kleinen Bruder.

Schreib **vier** Sätze auf **Deutsch** über das Foto.

(8 marks)

Exam-style question

Du schreibst an deine deutsche Freundin über deine Schule.

Schreib etwas über:

- dein Lieblingsfach
- ein Schulfach, das du **nicht** magst
- die Schulordnung
- Essen und Trinken in der Schule

Du musst ungefähr **40** Wörter auf **Deutsch** schreiben.

(16 marks)

How confident do you feel about each of these **skills?** Colour 🖊 in the bars.

1 How do I add interest to my descriptions?

2 How do I make my descriptions more engaging?

3 How do I write more accurately?

② Making your meaning clear

This unit will help you learn how to make your meaning clear in German. The skills you will build are to:

- write clear sentences in German
- avoid being over-ambitious
- write logically.

In the exam, you will be asked to tackle a short writing task like the one below. This unit will prepare you to write your own responses to these questions.

Exam-style question

Du schreibst an deine deutsche Freundin über deine Freizeit.

Schreib etwas über:

- Sport
- Freunde
- Kino und Theater
- Fernsehen.

Du musst ungefähr **40** Wörter auf **Deutsch** schreiben.

(16 marks)

The three key questions in the **skills boosts** will help you make your meaning clear.

 1 How do I write clear sentences in German?

 2 How do I avoid being over-ambitious?

 3 How do I write logically?

Look at the sample student response to this task on the next page.

Read one student's answer to the question on page 9.

> Ich bin ziemlich sportlich. Ich trainiere einmal pro Woche im Verein. Ich fahre am Samstag in die Stadt und ich treffe Freunde. Ich gehe oft ins Kino, aber ich mag das Theater nicht. Zu Hause sehe ich gern fern. Das kostet nichts!

1 Read these statements and tick ✓ three things that are mentioned in the student's answer above.

a going into town ☐

b swimming ☐

c buying CDs ☐

d going to the cinema ☐

e something that's expensive ☐

f being in a club ☐

2 **a** Look again at the answer. Write ✏ the German verbs that this student has used to respond to each bullet point in the question.

    i Sport ....

    ii Freunde ....

    iii Kino und Theater ....

    iv Fernsehen ....

  b Which of these verbs is **not** in the first person singular (*ich*) form?

    ....

3 Look at these questions. Find the phrase or sentence that answers each question in the student's response above and write it ✏ next to the question.

  a Wann fährst du in die Stadt? ....

  b Wie oft trainierst du? ....

  c Was machst du gern zu Hause? ....

  d Was machst du in der Stadt? ....

  e Was magst du nicht? ....

How do I write clear sentences in German?

To write clear sentences in German:

- make sure you do not miss out any key words
- make sure it is clear where one sentence ends and the next one begins.

Look again at the exam-style question on page 9.

1 Here are some sentences that students have written in response to the task. In each sentence a key word has been left out. Correct ✐ each sentence by inserting the missing word and then translate ✐ it into English.

a Ich interessiere ^mich^ für Theater.

....

b Samstagabend gehe ich oft ins Kino.

....

c Ich in einer Mannschaft gespielt.

....

d Ich spiele einmal Woche Hockey.

....

e Ich nicht gern fern.

....

f Ich turne drei Jahren.

....

2 Look at this response to the exam-style question on page 9. Add a forward slash ✐ to show where each full stop should go, and add capital letters ✐ where necessary.

> Ich bin sehr sportlich ich spiele seit fünf Jahren Fußball und trainiere oft ich habe viele
>
> Freunde wir gehen am Samstag in die Stadt das kino ist gut und ich mag das Theater zu Hause
>
> gucke ich amerikanische Filme auf meinem Tablet das ist toll!

3 Rewrite ✐ these jumbled sentences with the words in the correct order. Make sure you use a capital letter on the first word and a full stop at the end.

a spiele ich Tennis gern ....

b meine treffe Freunde ich ....

c ins gehen wir Kino ....

d meine sieht fern gern Schwester ....

....

e möchte fahren ich Skateboard ....

....

2 How do I avoid being over-ambitious?

Sometimes you will need to simplify your ideas so that you can say them correctly in German. Follow these two golden rules:

- stick to German that you know
- do not translate word for word from English.

1 Look at the sentences below. On the left are some ideas that a student would like to write about. On the right are simpler versions of these ideas in German. Draw lines ✏ to show which ideas go together.

A I get bored when playing online games.	a Ich spiele seit drei Wochen Klavier.
B I took up the piano three weeks ago.	b Ich gehe nicht gern einkaufen.
C I'd rather do anything than shopping.	c Ich möchte auf einen Weihnachtsmarkt gehen.
D Watching the news isn't too bad.	d Ich spiele nicht gern Computerspiele.
E A Christmas market is top of my wish list.	e Ich sehe ziemlich gern die Nachrichten.

2 Complete ✏ the German sentences to get across each idea more simply.

a I'd rather do anything than listen to music.   Ich höre .... Musik.

b My laptop is really handy for watching films.   Ich .... gern Filme auf meinem Laptop.

c Romantic films are not my thing.   Ich sehe .... gern Liebesfilme.

d Shopping is something I do on Saturdays.   Ich gehe .... einkaufen.

3 Dictionaries can be dangerous! In each of the sentences below the student has found two possible German translations for an English word or phrase. Circle Ⓐ the one that is correct. Then write ✏ the English word that you think the student was looking up.

a Wir **trainieren / Zug** einmal pro Woche auf dem Fußballplatz. ....

b **Schutzanzug / Im Großen und Ganzen** finde ich Computer positiv. ....

c Ich spiele oft Computerspiele auf meinem **Tablet / Schreibblock**. ....

d Ich spiele Geige und mein Bruder spielt **Aufnahmegerät / Blockflöte**. ....

e Ich kaufe **jetzt und dann / ab und zu** Kleidung. ....

f Zu Weihnachten **chille / kühle** ich gern mit Freunden. ....

③ How do I write logically?

Sometimes students write sentences where the individual words are correct, but the answer as a whole doesn't make sense. Make sure you:

- use conjunctions such as *aber* and *und* correctly
- only join ideas in one sentence if they are about related ideas
- write in a logical order.

> Use *aber* for contrasting two things and *und* for listing similar things.

① Do the sentences need *und* or *aber*? Write 🖉 your choice in the gap. Then translate 🖉 each sentence into English.

a Die Sendung war interessant .... unrealistisch.

....

> Make sure you place a comma before *aber*, but no comma before *und*.

b Ich spiele gern Handball .... fahre gern Ski.

....

c Wir sitzen um den Weihnachtsbaum .... öffnen Geschenke.*

....

> *öffnen Geschenke = open presents

d Kurt hört gern Rapmusik .... er ist noch nie auf ein Konzert gegangen.

....

② Look at the sentences below. Explain 🖉 in English what is wrong with each one.

a Ich treibe Sport und habe Computerspiele gespielt.

The two topics are unrelated and the tenses are different.

b Ich mag Opernmusik nicht, aber meine Musiksammlung* ist auf meinem Tablet.

> *die Musiksammlung = music collection

....

c Die Eintrittskarten sind teuer, denn Rapmusik ist besser.

....

d Wir gehen nie einkaufen und wir kaufen am liebsten Bücher.

....

③ Expand this student's notes using the sentences below. Decide where each sentence would fit logically and write 🖉 the letter in the box.

---

1 Ich verbringe viel Zeit am Computer. ☐   **2** Musik ist mir wichtig. ☐   **3** Ich gehe gar nicht gern einkaufen. ☐   **4** Ich feiere gern Weihnachten mit meiner Familie. ☐

A Ich bin gestern auf ein tolles Konzert gegangen.

C Ich surfe oder chatte gern im Internet.

B Ich finde das langweilig.

D Wir geben und bekommen Geschenke.

Sample response

To make your meaning clear, you need to:
- write clear sentences in German
- avoid being over-ambitious
- write logically.

Read Heidi's answer to the exam-style task you saw on page 9.

> Ich bin sportlich. Ich fahre am Samstag in die Stadt, aber ich treffe Freunde. Ich trainiere einmal pro Woche im Verein. Ich gehe oft Kino, denn ich mag das Theater. Zu Hause habe ich gern ferngesehen, das ist nicht köstlich!

1 First, check that you understand the German. Tick ✓ all the things that Heidi has included in her answer.

a her favourite sport ☐   **d** how often she goes to the theatre ☐

b when she goes to town ☐   **e** her opinion of TV ☐

c how often she goes to the cinema ☐

2 When checking her work, Heidi made a list of all the mistakes she found. Find each of these errors in Heidi's answer and explain ✏ what is wrong each time.

Illogical order of sentences: _The third sentence is about sport so belongs after the first sentence._

Incorrect use of *und* or *aber*: ....

....

Unrelated ideas in the same sentence: ....

Incorrect use of *denn*: ....

Missed out a key word: ....

Inappropriate use of tense: ....

Need to start a new sentence: ....

....

Incorrect adjective used: ....

3 Rewrite ✏ Heidi's answer to make it clearer.

....

....

....

....

Your turn!

You are now going to plan your response to this exam-style task.

Exam-style question

Du schreibst an deinen Schweizer Freund über deine Freizeit.

Schreib etwas über:

- Fernsehen

- Musik

- Partys

- Lesen.

Du musst ungefähr **40** Wörter auf **Deutsch** schreiben.

(16 marks)

1 Plan your answer. Think of two things to write about each bullet point. Write 🖉 key words and phrases in German in the table.

Bullet point	Idea 1	Idea 2
Fernsehen		
Musik		
Partys		
Lesen		

2 Using your ideas from **1**, write 🖉 your response to the exam-style question above. Then check your work with the checklist.

Checklist	✓
In my answer do I ...	
include key words?	
write in sentences?	
use German I know?	
simplify my ideas?	
use conjunctions *aber* and *und* correctly?	
join ideas in a sentence if they are related?	
write in a logical order?	

Review your skills

Check up

Review your response to the exam-style question on page 15. Tick ✓ the column to show how well you think you have done each of the following.

	Not quite ✓	Nearly there ✓	Got it! ✓
written clear sentences in German	☐	☐	☐
avoided being over-ambitious	☐	☐	☐
written logically	☐	☐	☐

Need more practice?

Plan and write 🖊 on paper your response to the task below.

Exam-style question

Du schreibst an deinen deutschen Freund über deine Freizeit.

Schreib etwas über:

• das Internet

• Lesen

• Freunde

• Feiern.

Du musst ungefähr **40** Wörter auf **Deutsch** schreiben.

(16 marks)

How confident do you feel about each of these **skills**? Colour 🖊 in the bars.

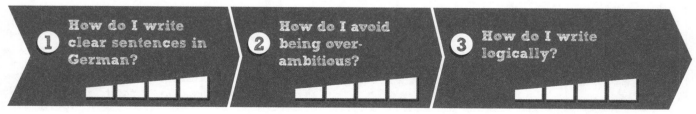

1 How do I write clear sentences in German?

2 How do I avoid being over-ambitious?

3 How do I write logically?

③ Improving your accuracy

This unit will help you learn how to improve your accuracy when writing in German. The skills you will build are to:

* improve the accuracy of verb and case endings
* improve the accuracy of word order
* improve spelling.

In the exam, you will be asked to tackle a short writing task like the one below. This unit will prepare you to write your own responses to these questions.

Exam-style question

Du schreibst an deine österreichische Freundin über Familie und Freunde.

Schreib etwas über:

* deine beste Freundin / deinen besten Freund – Aussehen
* deine beste Freundin / deinen besten Freund – Charaktereigenschaften
* deine Familienmitglieder – gute Beziehungen
* deine Familienmitglieder – schlechte Beziehungen.

Du musst ungefähr **40** Wörter auf **Deutsch** schreiben.

(16 marks)

The three key questions in the **skills boosts** will help you improve your accuracy.

 1 How do I improve the accuracy of my verb and case endings?

 2 How do I improve the accuracy of my word order?

 3 How do I improve my spelling?

Look at the sample student response to this task on the next page.

Exam-style question

Du schreibst an deine österreichische Freundin über Familie und Freunde.
Schreib etwas über:

- deine beste Freundin / deinen besten Freund – Aussehen
- deine beste Freundin / deinen besten Freund – Charaktereigenschaften
- deine Familienmitglieder – gute Beziehungen
- deine Familienmitglieder – schlechte Beziehungen.

Du musst ungefähr **40** Wörter auf **Deutsch** schreiben.

Remember that Freund can mean friend or boyfriend, and Freundin can mean friend or girlfriend.

(16 marks)

Meine beste Freundin heißt Sam. Sie hat lange, schwarze Haare und ist hübsch. Sie ist freundlich und sympathisch, aber nicht sportlich. Ich verstehe mich gut mit meinem Vater, weil er lustig ist, aber leider verstehe ich mich nicht so gut mit meiner Mutter.

---

1 Read the student's answer above. Tick ✓ three things that the student has mentioned.

a best friend's name ☐   **d** father's appearance ☐

b best friend's appearance ☐   **e** reason for good relationship with father ☐

c best friend's hobbies ☐   **f** reason for poor relationship with mother ☐

2 **a** Look again at the student's answer. Write ✐ the German adjectives and adverbs that the student has used to respond to each bullet point in the question.

   i deine beste Freundin / dein bester Freund – Aussehen

    lange, ...

   ii deine beste Freundin / dein bester Freund – Charaktereigenschaften

    ....

   iii deine Familienmitglieder – gute Beziehungen

    ....

   iv deine Familienmitglieder – schlechte Beziehungen

    ....

 b How can you tell that Sam is a girl? Write down ✐ the words in the student's answer that tell you this.

   ....

3 Look at these English phrases and find the German equivalent for each in the student's answer above. Write ✐ the German phrase next to the English.

 a my best friend ....

 b with my father ....

 c with my mother ....

How do I improve the accuracy of my verb and case endings?

To improve the accuracy of your writing you need to:

• use the correct verb endings
• use the correct endings on indefinite articles ('a') and possessive adjectives ('my', 'your', etc.) depending on the gender and the case.

1 Read the sentences below.

• Circle Ⓐ the article or possessive adjective in each sentence.

• Write ✏️ the case (nominative, accusative or dative) in the second column.

Remember your cases:
nominative case = subject
accusative case = direct object and after certain prepositions
dative case = indirect object and after certain prepositions

• Then write ✏️ the gender (masculine or feminine) or plural in the third column.

a Ich habe (einen) Bruder.   *accusative*   *masculine*

b Wir wohnen bei unserem Stiefvater. ....

c Meine Freunde sind sehr nett.   ....

d Ich verstehe mich gut mit meiner Mutter. ....

2 In these sentences the word in **bold** has the wrong ending. Write ✏️ each word correctly.

Endings of most verbs in the present tense:
ich	−e	wir	−en
du	−st	ihr	−t
er/sie/es	−t	Sie/sie	−en

Remember that the *ich* and *er/sie/es* forms of modal verbs do not have these endings, and that *sein* is irregular in all its forms.

a Mein bester Freund ~~heiße~~ *heißt* Niko.

b Meine beste Freundin **haben** kurze Haare.

Verbs: Think about the subject. *Mein bester Freund* is a 'he' and *Meine beste Freundin* is a 'she'. So both of these need a verb in the *er/sie/es* form.

c Mein Bruder und ich **verbringe** unsere Freizeit in der Stadt.

Mein Bruder und ich means 'my brother and I'. Which verb form do you need?

d Ich verstehe mich gut mit **meine** Oma.

Case endings: Check which case you need after prepositions – *mit* always takes the dative.

e **Meine** Opa hat viel Geduld.

f Ich liebe **meinen** Großeltern.

3 Here you need to identify the word with the wrong ending in each sentence. Write ✏️ each word correctly and explain why you have made the change.

a ~~Mein~~ *Meine* beste Freundin heißt Sara. *'Freundin' is feminine and in the nominative case.* ....

b Sara hast schwarze Haare. ....

c Ich gehe mit mein Freund in die Stadt. ....

② How do I improve the accuracy of my word order?

Remember the three main rules of German word order:

- In most sentences the verb is the second idea.
- A modal verb, like *muss* or *kann*, sends the infinitive verb to the end of the clause.
- After subordinating conjunctions, like *weil* and *als*, the verb goes to the end of the clause.

① Read these sentences about friends and family life. In each sentence the verb in **bold** is in the wrong place. Draw 🖉 an arrow to show where it should be. Then write 🖉 the sentences in English.

a Bastian und ich gute Freunde **sind**.

Bastian and I are good friends.
....

b Im Sommer wir **spielen** Tennis.

....

> *Im Sommer* is the first idea in this sentence.

c Ich kann **reden** mit Paula über alles.

....

> Notice the modal verb in this sentence.

d Ich mag Lotte, weil sie **ist** lustig.

....

> Remember that *weil* is a subordinating conjunction.

e Am Wochenende ich Computerspiele spielen **darf**.

....

f Meine Mutter war streng, als ich **war** elf Jahre alt.

....

② This time you need to identify the verb that is in the wrong place. Circle Ⓐ the verb and draw 🖉 an arrow to show where it should be. Then translate 🖉 each sentence into English.

a Tobias immer Zeit für mich (hat). *Tobias always has time for me.*

b Ich kann spielen mit Tobias Fußball. ....

c Heute ich verstehe mich gut mit meiner Stiefmutter. ....

....

d Wir viel Zeit zusammen verbringen. ....

e Sie war streng, als ich war ein Kind. ....

f Ich durfte kommen nicht spät nach Hause. ....

....

③ How do I improve my spelling?

German spelling is much more regular and predictable than English spelling, but you need to take care to avoid common pitfalls such as:

- confusion between *ei* and *ie*
- using umlauts incorrectly
- missing off capital letters on nouns.

① **a** Read what this student has written about friends and comparing life as a child to life now. Eleven incorrect words are highlighted. Underline Ⓐ the words where she has missed out a capital letter. Circle Ⓐ the words with a spelling mistake (an umlaut missed out, or an *ei* and *ie* mixed up).

> *Ein guter freund darf nie eifersuchtig sein. Mein bester Freund hat immer zeit für mich. Wir konnen uber alles reden. Ich hatte eine sehr schone kindheit. Ich durfte jeden tag in den Park gehen. Heute leibe ich Fußball und ich traineire oft.*

To help you work out if you need *ie* or *ei*, say the word aloud. If it sounds like 'ee' in English, you need *ie*. If it sounds like 'eye' in English, you need *ei*.

b Write 🖉 the correct spellings of the highlighted words.

....

....

....

....

You will only find an umlaut on the vowels a, o and u (ä, ö, ü). The vowels e and i never have an umlaut in German.

Other common spelling errors include:
- missing out letters (such as the 'c' in the German *sch*)
- writing letters the wrong way round (such as writing 'ue' instead of 'eu' in words like *Freund*)
- misspelling near-cognates (words that are like the English – such as writing 'Garden' instead of *Garten*).

② **a** The student's answer below contains six spelling mistakes. The first one has already been identified. Underline Ⓐ the five remaining misspelled words.

> *Ich **vebringe** viel Zeit mit meinen Freundinnen und Fruenden. Wir sind sehr active. Wir spielen Tennis und gehen shwimmen. Ich mache auch viel mit meiner Family. Wir gehen einkaufen und farhen ab und zu Rad.*

b Write 🖉 the correct spellings of the words you identified.

verbringe
....

....

Sample response

To improve your accuracy, you need to:

- improve the accuracy of your verb and case endings
- improve the accuracy of your word order
- improve your spelling.

Read Oli's answer to this exam-style task. Has he followed all the advice about improving his accuracy?

Exam-style question

Du schreibst an deine österreichische Freundin über Familie und Freunde.

Schreib etwas über:

- deine beste Freundin / deinen besten Freund – Aussehen
- deine beste Freundin / deinen besten Freund – Charaktereigenschaften
- deine Familienmitglieder – gute Beziehungen
- deine Familienmitglieder – schlechte Beziehungen.

Du musst ungefähr **40** Wörter auf **Deutsch** schreiben.   (16 marks)

---

spelling error
Mein bester <u>Fruend</u> ist intelligent und sehr nett. Er ist <u>shlank</u> und hat kurze <u>haare</u> und

braune Augen. Wir <u>hat</u> die gleichen Interessen. Ich verstehe mich auch gut mit <u>mein</u> Stiefvater. Ich

kann <u>reden</u> mit ihm <u>uber</u> alles. Aber meine <u>Muter</u> geht mir auf die Nerven, weil sie <u>ist</u> immer <u>fleißig</u>.

---

1 First, check that you understand the German. Read these statements and tick ✓ all the things that Oli has mentioned.

a best friend's appearance ☐   **d** why he gets on with his stepdad ☐

b best friend's personality ☐   **e** why his mum annoys him ☐

c stepdad's appearance ☐   **f** an activity he does with his mum ☐

2 The underlined words in the student's answer have been written incorrectly. Annotate ✐ these words, stating the type of error: wrong ending, word order error, spelling error or missing capital letter.

3 Rewrite ✐ Oli's answer to make it more accurate.

....

....

....

....

....

Your turn!

You are now going to plan and write your response to this exam-style task.

Du schreibst an deinen Schweizer Freund über Familie und Freunde.

Schreib etwas über:

- Freundinnen/Freunde – was ist wichtig?

- Aktivitäten mit Freundinnen/Freunden

- Beziehungen zu Familienmitgliedern

- Aktivitäten mit der Familie.

Du musst ungefähr **40** Wörter auf **Deutsch** schreiben.   **(16 marks)**

1 Plan your answer. Think of two things to write about each bullet point. Write 🖋 key words and phrases in German in the table.

Bullet point	Idea 1	Idea 2
Freundinnen/Freunde – was ist wichtig?		
Aktivitäten mit Freundinnen/Freunden		
Beziehungen zu Familienmitgliedern		
Aktivitäten mit der Familie		

2 Using your ideas from **1**, write 🖋 your response to the exam-style question above. Then check your work with the checklist.

Checklist	✓
In my answer do I ...	
use the correct verb endings?	
use the correct case endings?	
have a verb as the second idea?	
use modal verbs with an infinitive at the end?	
use subordinating conjunctions with a verb at the end?	
use *ei* and *ie* correctly?	
use umlauts correctly?	
remember to put capital letters on nouns?	
avoid missing out any letters?	
position all the letters the right way round?	
avoid using near-cognates wrongly?	

Review your skills

Check up

Review your response to the exam-style question on page 23. Tick ✓ the column to show how well you think you have done each of the following.

	Not quite ✓	Nearly there ✓	Got it! ✓
used the correct verb endings and case endings	☐	☐	☐
got the word order right	☐	☐	☐
spelled words correctly	☐	☐	☐

Need more practice?

On paper, plan and write ✏ your response to the task below.

Exam-style question

Du schreibst an deinen deutschen Freund über Familie und Freunde.

Schreib etwas über:

- Familienmitglieder – Aussehen
- Familienmitglieder – gute und schlechte Beziehungen
- Freundinnen/Freunde – Charaktereigenschaften
- Aktivitäten mit Freundinnen/Freunden.

Du musst ungefähr **40** Wörter auf **Deutsch** schreiben.

(16 marks)

How confident do you feel about each of these **skills?** Colour ✏ in the bars.

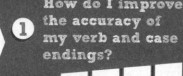
1 How do I improve the accuracy of my verb and case endings?

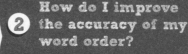
2 How do I improve the accuracy of my word order?

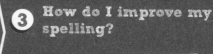
3 How do I improve my spelling?

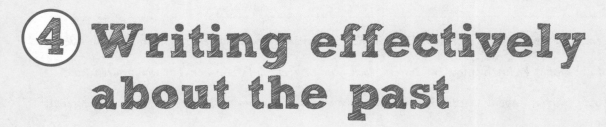

④ Writing effectively about the past

This unit will help you learn how to write effectively about things that happened in the past. The skills you will build are to:

• use opportunities to write about the past
• vary your references to the past to add interest
• ensure that your past tense verbs are correct.

In the exam, you will be asked to tackle a writing task like the one below. This unit will prepare you to write your own responses to these questions.

Exam-style question

Dein Freund Timo aus Österreich kommt bald zu dir. Er hat dich nach deinem Zuhause gefragt. Du schreibst Timo eine E-Mail über dein Zuhause.

Schreib:

• etwas über dein Haus oder deine Wohnung

• warum du gern oder nicht gern dort wohnst

• was du letztes Wochenende zu Hause gemacht hast

• etwas über deine Pläne für seinen Besuch.

Du musst ungefähr **90** Wörter auf **Deutsch** schreiben. Schreib etwas über alle Punkte der Aufgabe.

(16 marks)

The three key questions in the **skills boosts** will help you write effectively about the past.

1 How do I use opportunities to write about the past?

2 How do I vary my references to the past to add interest?

3 How do I ensure that my past tense verbs are correct?

Look at the sample student response to this task on the next page.

> Ich wohne mit meiner Familie in einem Haus in der Stadtmitte. Im Erdgeschoss haben wir eine kleine Küche und ein großes Wohnzimmer. Im ersten Stock gibt es drei Schlafzimmer. Ich wohne gern hier, weil wir einen Garten haben. Letztes Wochenende war ich am Samstag zu Hause. Ich habe ferngesehen und eine Zeitschrift gelesen. Zwei Freunde sind auch zu mir gekommen und wir haben Tischtennis gespielt. Das hat Spaß gemacht. Wenn du zu Besuch bist, werden wir im Garten Fußball spielen und wir werden auch einkaufen gehen. Die Geschäfte sind in der Nähe.

1 Read Oliver's answer to the writing task from page 25 and answer ✐ these questions in English.

a Where is Oliver's house? ....

b Which rooms are there on the ground floor? ....

c How many bedrooms are there? ....

d What did Oliver do last Saturday? (three activities)

....

e What activities are planned for when Timo comes to visit? (two activities)

....

f Where are the shops? ....

2 Look at these extracts from Oliver's answer above. Decide whether each extract is referring to the present, the past or the future. Tick ✓ the appropriate column.

	Present ✓	Past ✓	Future ✓
a Ich wohne mit meiner Familie in einem Haus ...			
b Im ersten Stock gibt es drei Schlafzimmer.			
c Letztes Wochenende war ich am Samstag zu Hause.			
d Ich habe ferngesehen ...			
e ... wir haben Tischtennis gespielt.			
f ... wir werden auch einkaufen gehen.			
g Die Geschäfte sind in der Nähe.			

3 **a** Now circle Ⓐ all six past tense verbs in Oliver's answer.

b What is the tense of the verbs you have circled? Above each verb, write ✐ imperfect or perfect.

> Remember the two tenses you can use to refer to the past.
> • Imperfect tense verbs are just one word: *war, gab*, etc.
> • Perfect tense verbs have two parts: *habe ... gespielt, bin ... gegangen*, etc.

1 How do I use opportunities to write about the past?

In the 90-word writing question, one of the bullet points will normally require an answer referring to the past. Make sure you spot which bullet point this is before you start writing. You may also refer to the past in response to other bullet points if you wish.

1 **a** Look at these bullet points, which could appear in an exam question. Tick ✓ the three bullet points that require an answer in the past.

- was du jeden Tag isst und trinkst ☐
- wo du wohnst ☐
- was du gestern gegessen hast ☐
- was du letztes Wochenende gemacht hast ☐
- wie viele Stunden du in der Schule verbringst ☐
- was du nicht machen durftest, als du jünger warst ☐

b Circle Ⓐ the past tense verb(s) in each of the bullet points you have chosen.

2 Make your writing about the past more specific by using appropriate time phrases. Draw lines ✎ to match these German time phrases with their English translations. Tick ✓ the German phrase that **can only** be used with a past tense verb.

A am Nachmittag	a when I was younger
B heute	b at half past eight
C um 8 Uhr 30	c today
D als ich jünger war	d in the afternoon

3 Look again at the three bullet points you identified in **1**. Underline Ⓐ the time phrase in each one.

4 Rewrite ✎ these perfect tense sentences, using a different time phrase each time. Choose from the box or use your own ideas.

~~Letztes Wochenende~~	Am Samstag	Am Sonntagmorgen	Letzte Woche	Gestern
Am Nachmittag				

Use the correct word order. The auxiliary verb (the part of *haben* or *sein*) must be the second idea, so it comes straight after the time phrase. The past participle goes at the end as usual.

a Ich habe gefaulenzt. _Letztes Wochenende habe ich gefaulenzt._

b Ich habe ein Buch gelesen. ....

c Wir sind Rad gefahren. ....

d Ich bin zu Hause geblieben. ....

5 Write ✎ four sentences on paper to answer the question *Was hast du letztes Wochenende zu Hause gemacht?* Use sentences from this page or your own ideas.

② How do I vary my references to the past to add interest?

You can vary your references to the past by:

- using different persons of the verb (*wir* and *er/sie/es* as well as *ich*)
- adding sentences in the imperfect tense (*ich war, sie hatte, es gab ...,* etc.)
- using a range of different verbs.

① Practise using different persons of the verb. Rewrite ✏ each of the following sentences starting with the given person. Use the appropriate part of *haben* or *sein* from the box.

| ich habe | du hast | er/sie/es hat | wir haben | ihr habt | Sie haben | sie haben |
| ich bin | du bist | er/sie/es ist | wir sind | ihr seid | Sie sind | sie sind |

a Ich habe ferngesehen. _Meine Schwester hat ferngesehen._

b Ich habe ein Buch gelesen. _Mein Bruder_

c Ich habe Apfelsaft getrunken. _Sila und Gregor_

d Ich habe laute Musik gespielt. _Wir_

e Ich habe eine E-Mail geschrieben. _Du_

f Ich bin in die Küche gegangen. _Der Hund_

② Practise using the imperfect tense forms *war* and *waren*. Draw lines ✏ between the columns to make sentences. Then translate the sentences into English.

> Remember that *war* is singular and *waren* is plural.

A Die Musik		a war sehr klein.	
B Die Nachrichten		b waren streng.	
C Mein Zimmer		c war laut.	
D Die Eltern		d waren interessant.	

③ Complete ✏ this student's description of lunch at her exchange partner's house in Switzerland using the perfect and imperfect tenses. Use verbs from the box below.

| haben | hat | sind | spielen | war | waren |
| durfte | gegangen | gegessen | geschmeckt | getrunken | habe |

Um ein Uhr (a) .... wir zu Mittag (b) .... Fisch und Schnitzel (c) .... auf der Karte. Ich (d) .... Milch (e) .... Das Mittagessen (f) .... wunderbar (g) .... Der Fisch (h) .... besonders köstlich. Nach dem Essen (i) .... wir ins Wohnzimmer (j) .... Ich (k) .... keine Computerspiele (l) ....

③ How do I ensure that my past tense verbs are correct?

Check to make sure you have written the perfect tense correctly:

• Does the verb take *haben* or *sein*?	Most take *haben* but verbs involving movement such as *fahren*, *gehen*, *fliegen* and *kommen* take *sein*.
• Have I used the correct part of *haben* or *sein*?	It must agree with the subject.
• Have I used the correct past participle?	Past participles end in *-t* or *-en* and often start with *ge-*. Make sure you learn the common irregular past participles.
• Have I used the right word order?	The past participle comes at the end of the phrase or sentence.

① **a** Look at these sentences that a student has written about his first evening on an exchange visit to Germany. Identify what is missing in each sentence: is it a past participle, a form of *haben* or a form of *sein*? Write ✎ PP, H or S in the box.

i Ich .... um sechs Uhr angekommen. ☐

ii Niklas hat mir mein Zimmer .... ☐

iii Seine Eltern .... mit mir gesprochen. ☐

iv Ich .... nicht alles verstanden. ☐

v Dann haben wir Abendbrot .... ☐

vi Niklas .... am Computer gespielt. ☐

vii Um elf Uhr .... wir ins Bett gegangen. ☐

b Now complete the sentences above by writing ✎ the correct word from the box in each gap.

habe	haben	hat	bin	sind	gezeigt	gegessen

② Read this student's paragraph about an exchange visit. She has made seven mistakes with verbs referring to the past. Underline Ⓐ the mistakes and write ✎ the correct version above the word.

> Make sure you know the imperfect tense forms of *haben*, *sein* and the modal verbs. You also need to know *es gab* (there was/were).

Am Samstag waren ich zu Hause mit meiner Austauschpartnerin, Zehra. Wir haben Tischtennis gespielen. Das ist Spaß gemacht. Danach habe ich ein Buch gelesen und Zehra hast Musik gehört. Wir haben dann zu Mittag essen. Es gibt Wurst mit Kartoffeln und Gemüse. Das haben sehr gut geschmeckt.

A common mistake is to use the present tense instead of a past tense. Can you spot where this has happened in this student's writing?

Sample response

To write effectively about the past, you need to:

- use opportunities to write about the past
- vary your references to the past to add interest
- ensure that your past tense verbs are correct.

Look at this new exam-style writing task and the student's answer below.

Exam-style question

Deine Freundin Sofia aus Deutschland hat dich nach deinem Tagesablauf gefragt. Du schreibst ihr eine E-Mail.

Schreib:

- etwas über deinen Tagesablauf an einem Schultag
- was du am Abend zu Hause machst
- was du gestern gegessen und getrunken hast
- etwas über deine Pläne für nächstes Wochenende.

> The third bullet point is about what you ate and drank yesterday so you need to use past tenses to answer it.

Du musst ungefähr **90** Wörter auf **Deutsch** schreiben. Schreib etwas über alle Punkte der Aufgabe.

(16 marks)

An einem Schultag stehe ich um halb acht auf. Ich frühstücke in der Küche und dann gehe ich zur Schule. Am Abend mache ich immer meine Hausaufgaben. Dann bin ich müde und ich sehe gern fern, aber gestern hatte ich keine Hausaufgaben und ich habe am Computer gespielt. Gestern Abend habe ich Currywurst gegessen. Sie hat lecker geschmeckt, weil sie würzig war. Ich habe kein Gemüse gegessen, denn ich mag das nicht. Nächstes Wochenende werde ich Musik auf meinem Tablet hören und einen Film sehen. Ich werde vielleicht mit meinem Bruder Gitarre spielen.

> This student has also spotted an opportunity to use past tenses to talk about the activities she did yesterday evening, although the second bullet point doesn't specifically ask for this.

1 Look at the verbs in the student's answer. Circle (A) all the verbs referring to the past. Write down (✏) their English translations.

> Remember that perfect tense verbs consist of two words.

....

....

2 a The student missed out part of one of the bullet points. What did she miss out? (✏)

....

b Write (✏) a sentence in German to cover this point.

....

3 Write (✏) three past tense sentences of your own on paper to answer the third bullet point. Use a range of pronouns or nouns as well as *ich*. Make sure the verbs agree.

Your turn!

You are now going to plan and write your response to this exam-style task.

Dein Freund Paul aus der Schweiz interessiert sich für Technologie und hat dich danach gefragt. Du schreibst ihm eine E-Mail über Technologie.

Schreib:

- wie du das Internet benutzt

- wie du letzte Woche dein Handy benutzt hast

- wie du soziale Netzwerke findest, und warum

- wie du nächste Woche mit deinen Freundinnen/Freunden kommunizieren wirst.

Du musst ungefähr **90** Wörter auf **Deutsch** schreiben. Schreib etwas über alle Punkte der Aufgabe.

> You will need to use the past tenses to answer the second bullet point. You can also make references to the past in response to the other bullet points, but you don't have to.

(16 marks)

(1) Plan your answer. Think of two things to write about each bullet point. Write 🖊 key words and phrases in German. Make sure the verbs are in the appropriate tense.

- wie du das Internet benutzt ....

....

....

- wie du letzte Woche dein Handy benutzt hast ....

....

....

- wie du soziale Netzwerke findest und warum ....

....

....

- wie du nächste Woche mit deinen Freundinnen/Freunden kommunizieren wirst ....

....

....

(2) Now write 🖊 your response to the above exam-style question on paper, using the checklist to help you.

Checklist	✓		✓
In my answer do I ...		use a range of different verbs?	
identify which bullet point refers to the past?		use *haben*, *sein* and the correct past participles in perfect tense verbs?	
use past tense verbs to answer this bullet point?		use correct word order in perfect tense verbs?	
use different persons of the verb?		use the imperfect tense correctly?	
add sentences in the imperfect tense?		make sure my verbs agree with their subject?	

Review your skills

Check up

Review your response to the exam-style question on page 31. Tick ✓ the column to show how well you think you have done each of the following.

	Not quite ✓	Nearly there ✓	Got it! ✓
used opportunities to write about the past	☐	☐	☐
varied references to the past to add interest	☐	☐	☐
ensured past tense verbs are correct	☐	☐	☐

Need more practice?

On paper, plan and write ✏ your response to the task below.

Exam-style question

Deine Freundin Jasmin aus Deutschland lebt gern gesund und hat dich gefragt, ob du auch gesund lebst. Du schreibst ihr eine E-Mail.

Schreib etwas über:

• deine Fitness

• was du isst und trinkst und warum

• was du letzte Woche für deine Gesundheit gemacht hast

• was du nächste Woche für deine Gesundheit machen wirst.

Du musst ungefähr **90** Wörter auf **Deutsch** schreiben. Schreib etwas über alle Punkte der Aufgabe.

(16 marks)

How confident do you feel about each of these **skills?** Colour ✏ in the bars.

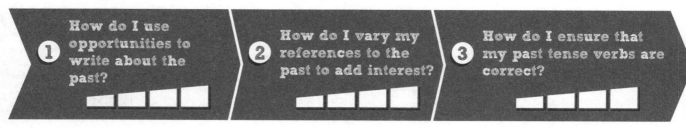

1 How do I use opportunities to write about the past?

2 How do I vary my references to the past to add interest?

3 How do I ensure that my past tense verbs are correct?

⑤ Writing effectively about the future

This unit will help you learn how to write effectively about the future. The skills you will build are to:

• use opportunities to write about the future

• vary your references to the future to add interest

• ensure that your verbs referring to the future are correct.

In the exam, you will be asked to tackle a writing task like the one below. This unit will prepare you to write your own responses to these questions.

Exam-style question

Du bist im Urlaub in einer Stadt. Du schreibst deiner österreichischen Freundin eine Postkarte über deinen Urlaub.

Schreib:

• etwas über die Reise

• etwas über die Unterkunft

• was du gestern in der Stadt gemacht hast

• was du morgen machen möchtest und warum.

Du musst ungefähr **90** Wörter auf **Deutsch** schreiben. Schreib etwas über alle Punkte der Aufgabe.

(16 marks)

The three key questions in the **skills boosts** will help you write effectively about the future.

 ① How do I use opportunities to write about the future?

 ② How do I vary my references to the future to add interest?

③ How do I ensure that my verbs referring to the future are correct?

Look at the sample student response to this task on the next page.

Here is one student's answer to the exam-style question on page 33.

> Ich bin mit meiner Familie in London. Wir sind mit dem Zug gefahren. Die Reise war schneller als mit dem Auto, aber sehr teuer. Wir übernachten in einem Hotel in der Stadtmitte. Das ist besser als eine Jugendherberge. Es gibt ein Restaurant und wir haben auch WLAN. Das ist praktisch, weil ich mein Tablet habe. Gestern haben wir viele Sehenswürdigkeiten gesehen und wir sind einkaufen gegangen. Ich habe ein Geschenk für meinen Freund gekauft. Morgen gehen wir in einen Andenkenladen, denn ich möchte Souvenirs kaufen. Wir werden auch ins Theater gehen. Das wird interessant sein.

1 **a** Read the student's answer above. Then read these statements and tick ✓ three things that the student has mentioned.

☐ cost of travel ....

☐ seeing the sights ....

☐ description of hotel room ....

☐ plan to visit a museum ....

☐ hotel Wi-Fi ....

☐ plan to go to a theme park ....

b Next to each statement you have ticked, note down 🖉 what the student has written about this aspect of her holiday.

2 Look at these extracts from the student's answer. Decide whether each extract is referring to the present, the past or the future. Tick ✓ the appropriate column.

	Present ✓	Past ✓	Future ✓
a Ich bin ... in London.	✓		
b Wir sind mit dem Zug gefahren.			
c Wir übernachten in einem Hotel ...			
d Gestern haben wir viele Sehenswürdigkeiten gesehen ...			
e Ich habe ein Geschenk ... gekauft.			
f ... ich möchte Souvenirs kaufen.			
g Das wird interessant sein.			

3 **a** Now circle Ⓐ all four verbs that refer to the future in the student's answer.

Remember that some of these verbs will consist of two words.

b Write down 🖉 the English meaning of each of the verbs you have circled on the lines below.

....

....

1 How do I use opportunities to write about the future?

In the 90-word writing question, one bullet point will normally require an answer referring to the future. Make sure you spot which bullet point this is before you start writing. You may also refer to the future in response to other bullet points if you wish.

1 Look at these bullet points, which could appear in an exam question. Tick ✓ the four bullet points that require an answer in the future.

> Remember that the present tense can be used to talk about the future, so the bullet point may not contain a future tense verb. Look for other future clues such as time phrases.

- etwas über deine Reise ☐
- wo du übernachten wirst ☐
- was du nächste Woche machst ☐
- etwas über die Unterkunft ☐

- was du am liebsten isst ☐
- wohin du morgen gehst ☐
- was du jeden Abend machst ☐
- deine Pläne für das Wochenende ☐

2 **a** In the table below, tick ✓ the appropriate column for each time phrase.

b Write ✏ the English meaning of each phrase in the final column.

	always refers to the future ✓	may refer to the future ✓	never refers to the future ✓	English meaning
am Wochenende				
nächsten Dienstag				
gestern				
wenn ich älter bin				
morgen früh				
um 5 Uhr 30				

3 Look at what a student has written about a planned trip to Berlin. Rewrite ✏ the sentences by changing the highlighted sections to talk about your own plans for a trip (real or imaginary).

a Nächste Woche fahre ich mit meinen Freunden nach Berlin. ....

....

b Wir werden mit dem Zug reisen. ....

c Am Samstag will ich die Sehenswürdigkeiten besichtigen. ....

....

d Ich möchte einkaufen gehen. ....

e Am Montag kommen wir nach Hause zurück. ....

....

② How do I vary my references to the future to add interest?

You can add interest to your writing by:

- using different ways of referring to the future, such as the future tense with *werden*, the present tense with a suitable time phrase, and a modal verb such as *möchte* or *wollen* + infinitive.

- using different persons of the verb (for example, *wir* and *er/sie/es* as well as *ich*).

---

1 Write ✏ sentences in the future tense using *werden* + infinitive with the phrases and the person given.

Remember the parts of *werden*:	
ich werde	*wir werden*
du wirst	*ihr werdet*
er/sie/es wird	*Sie/sie werden*

a schwimmen gehen (*ich*)   *Ich werde schwimmen gehen.*

b ins Restaurant gehen (*wir*) ....

c Tischtennis spielen (*Miriam*) ....

d um 13 Uhr ankommen (*meine Eltern*) ....

e das Museum besuchen (*ich*) ....

f interessant sein (*das*) ....

2 **a** Rewrite ✏ these sentences using a different way of referring to the future, as indicated by the sentence beginnings below.

    i Ich werde eine Stadtrundfahrt machen.

    Morgen *mache ich eine Stadtrundfahrt.* ....

    ii Morgen kaufe ich Souvenirs.

    Ich werde ....

    iii Nächstes Wochenende suchen wir Geschenke.

    Wir möchten ....

    iv Wir werden im Restaurant essen.

    Heute Abend ....

    v Am Sonntag geht meine Schwester schwimmen.

    Meine Schwester will ....

b Now, on paper, translate ✏ your sentences into English.

3 Here are two sentences a student has written to answer the question *Was wirst du in den Sommerferien machen?* Adapt ✏ them to talk about your own holiday plans.

a In den Sommerferien werde ich nach Italien fahren.

....

b Wir werden mit dem Flugzeug fliegen.

....

3 How do I ensure that my verbs referring to the future are correct?

- If the sentence has one verb (present tense referring to the future), check that it agrees with its subject: *ich fahre, er/sie/es fährt, wir fahren.*
- If the sentence has two verbs, the first verb agrees with its subject and the second verb is in the infinitive: *ich werde ... fahren, er/sie/es will ... fahren, wir möchten ... fahren.*

1 **a** Look at these sentences. Circle Ⓐ the correct form of the verb in bold.

    i   Ich werde nach Spanien **fliege / fliegen.**

    ii Morgen **übernachte / übernachten** wir im Hotel.

    iii Das **werde / wird** teuer sein.

    iv Ich möchte am liebsten in einer Jugendherberge **wohne / wohnen.**

    v Meine Mutter will im Restaurant **isst / essen.**

    vi Nächsten Mittwoch **gehe / gehen** ich schwimmen.

  b In five of the sentences, the verb has two parts. Underline Ⓐ the other part of the verb in each of these sentences.

2 Each of these sentences written by a student contains one verb in the wrong form. Underline Ⓐ that verb and write 🖉 the correct form at the end of the sentence.

  a | Wir werde den Bus nehmen. | ....

  b | Das Abendessen wird gut schmeckt. | ....

  c | Ich möchte Andenken kaufe. | ....

  d | Meine Schwester werden mit der Achterbahn fahren. | ....

  e | Wir übernachte morgen lieber in einer Hütte. | ....

  f | Im Sommer wollen wir mit dem Rad nach Italien fahre. | ....

3 Read this student's paragraph about his plans for a weekend in Stuttgart. He has made seven mistakes with verbs referring to the future. Underline Ⓐ the mistakes and write 🖉 the correct version above the word.

> Am Samstag fahre wir nach Stuttgart. Ich möchte in der Stadtmitte einkaufen
>
> gehe und mein Bruder will ein Museum besucht. Wir werde in einem Hotel
>
> übernachten. Das wird teuer sind. Am Sonntag möchten ich schwimmen gehen.
>
> Vielleicht esse wir am Sonntagabend in einem schönen Restaurant.

Sample response

To write effectively about the future, you need to:

- use opportunities to write about the future
- vary your references to the future to add interest
- ensure that your verbs referring to the future are correct.

Look at this new exam-style writing task and the student's answer below.

Exam-style question

Du bist im Urlaub in einer Stadt. Du schreibst deinem deutschen Freund eine Postkarte.

Schreib:

- wie du zur Stadt gefahren bist und warum

- etwas über das Essen

- was du in der Stadt gern oder nicht gern machst

- was du heute Abend machen möchtest und warum.

Du musst ungefähr **90** Wörter auf **Deutsch** schreiben. Schreib etwas über alle Punkte der Aufgabe.

(16 marks)

Ich bin mit meiner Familie in Edinburgh. Wir sind mit dem Auto nach Edinburgh gefahren, aber die Reise war sehr lang – sechs Stunden! Und es ist nicht so umweltfreundlich. Das Essen hier ist sehr gut. Morgen gehen wir ins Restaurant und ich werde Fisch mit Pommes essen. In der Stadt mache ich immer gern eine Stadtrundfahrt mit dem Bus, weil ich alles sehen kann und es nicht zu anstrengend ist. In Edinburgh gibt es viele Sehenswürdigkeiten. Aber ich gehe nicht gern einkaufen, denn ich finde Geschäfte so langweilig und die Souvenirs sind teuer.

> The second bullet point doesn't specifically refer to the future, but the student has spotted an opportunity to write about where he will go to eat tomorrow.

1 **a** Look at the verbs in the student's answer. Circle Ⓐ the two verbs referring to the future. Write ✐ the English translations of these verbs. ....

b One of these verbs is in the present tense. Underline Ⓐ the time phrase the student has used to show that he is referring to the future.

2 **a** The student missed out one of the bullet points. What did he miss out? ✐

....

b Read this possible answer to the missing bullet point, then write ✐ your own answer on paper.

Heute Abend gehen wir ins Konzert. Ich höre am liebsten Livemusik und das Konzert wird großartig sein. Dann möchte ich mit meinen Freunden im Internet chatten.

> To give an opinion about a future event, use: *Das wird [adjective] sein.* You could also add a qualifier such as *bestimmt* (definitely), *wahrscheinlich* (probably) or *vielleicht* (perhaps): *Das wird bestimmt toll sein.*

Your turn!

You are now going to plan and write your response to this exam-style task.

Du bist im Urlaub in einer Stadt. Du schreibst deinem Schweizer Freund Daniel eine Postkarte.

Schreib:

• etwas über die Reise

• warum du die Stadt magst oder nicht magst

• was du gestern Abend in der Stadt gemacht hast

• was du morgen machen möchtest und warum.

Du musst ungefähr **90** Wörter auf **Deutsch** schreiben. Schreib etwas
über alle Punkte der Aufgabe.

(16 marks)

1 Plan your answer. Think of two things to write about each bullet point. Write 🖉 key words and
phrases in German in the boxes.

Bullet point	Idea 1	Idea 2
etwas über die Reise		
warum du die Stadt magst oder nicht magst		
was du gestern Abend in der Stadt gemacht hast		
was du morgen machen möchtest und warum		

2 Now write 🖉 your response to the above exam-style question on paper, using the checklist to
help you.

Checklist	✓		✓
In my answer do I ...		use different persons of the verb?	
identify which bullet point refers to the future?		ensure that verbs with one part agree with the subject?	
use time phrases that refer to the future?		ensure that, in verbs with two parts, the part of *werden*, *möchte* or *wollen* agrees with the subject?	
use different ways of referring to the future?		ensure that, in verbs with two parts, the infinitive is at the end of the sentence?	

Review your skills

Check up

Review your response to the exam-style question on page 39. Tick ✓ the column to show how well you think you have done each of the following.

	Not quite ✓	Nearly there ✓	Got it! ✓
used opportunities to write about the future	☐	☐	☐
varied references to the future to add interest	☐	☐	☐
ensured verbs referring to the future are correct	☐	☐	☐

Need more practice?

On paper, plan and write ✏️ your response to the task below.

Exam-style question

Du bist im Urlaub in einer Stadt. Du schreibst deiner deutschen Freundin eine Postkarte.

Schreib:

• etwas über die Unterkunft

• was du isst und trinkst

• was du in der Stadt gesehen und gekauft hast

• was du heute Abend machen wirst und warum.

Du musst ungefähr **90** Wörter auf **Deutsch** schreiben. Schreib etwas über alle Punkte der Aufgabe.

(16 marks)

How confident do you feel about each of these **skills**? Colour ✏️ in the bars.

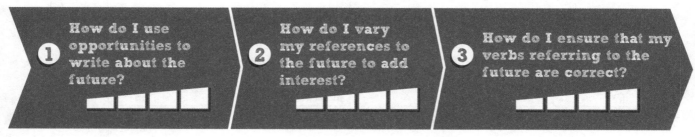

1 How do I use opportunities to write about the future?

2 How do I vary my references to the future to add interest?

3 How do I ensure that my verbs referring to the future are correct?

⑥ Choosing and linking your ideas

This unit will help you learn how to choose and link your ideas. The skills you will build are to:

- choose appropriate material using language that you know
- organise your writing
- use conjunctions appropriately.

In the exam, you will be asked to tackle a writing task like the one below. This unit will prepare you to write your own responses to these questions.

Exam-style question

Deine deutsche Freundin Finja hat dich nach deiner Stadt gefragt. Du schreibst Finja eine E-Mail über deine Stadt.

Schreib:

- etwas über die Vorteile deiner Stadt
- etwas über die Nachteile deiner Stadt
- was du letzte Woche in deiner Stadt gemacht hast
- wo du später wohnen möchtest und warum.

Du musst ungefähr **90** Wörter auf **Deutsch** schreiben. Schreib etwas über alle Punkte der Aufgabe.

(16 marks)

The three key questions in the **skills boosts** will help you choose and link your ideas.

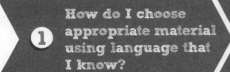

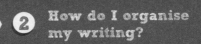

Look at the sample student response to this task on the next page.

> *Ich wohne in einer kleinen Stadt in Südwestengland. Ich mag meine Stadt, weil es viel zu tun gibt. Wir haben ein Kino, ein Schwimmbad und einen Park. Es wird ein Fußballstadion geben. Aber in meiner Stadt gibt es auch viel Verkehr und viel Lärm. Das ist ein großer Nachteil. Letzten Samstag bin ich mit meinem Bruder in die Stadtmitte gegangen. Ich habe Kleidung gekauft und wir haben in einem China-Restaurant gegessen. Mein Bruder hat nichts gekauft. Ich möchte später in Exeter wohnen, denn es gibt dort eine gute Universität. Ich will nicht auf dem Land wohnen.*

1 a First, make sure you understand the German. Tick ✓ the three things that are mentioned in the student's response.

reason for liking home town	☐	cycle paths	☐	reason for wanting to live in Exeter	☐
a future stadium	☐	a nearby airport	☐	a visit to the country	☐

b Tick ✓ the four statements that are true according to the student's answer above.

i   Ich wohne in Südwestengland. ☐

ii   Ich wohne in einer Großstadt. ☐

iii   In meiner Stadt gibt es nichts zu tun. ☐

iv   Ich gehe oft ins Fußballstadion. ☐

v   Ich mag den Lärm nicht. ☐

vi   Am Samstag bin ich ins Restaurant gegangen. ☐

vii   Mein Bruder hat Kleidung gekauft. ☐

viii   Exeter hat eine gute Universität. ☐

2 Look at how the student's answer is organised. Use four different coloured pens to highlight 🖉 the sentences that address each bullet point of the exam-style question on page 41.

3 a Find and circle Ⓐ these conjunctions in the student's response.

> aber   denn   und   und   weil

b Adapt some sentences from the student's response above. Complete 🖉 these sentences.

i   Ich mag meine Stadt, weil ....

ii   Aber in meiner Stadt gibt es auch ....

iii   Letzten Samstag bin ich mit .... gegangen.

iv   Ich habe .... und wir haben ....

v   Ich möchte später in .... wohnen, denn es gibt dort ....

....

① How do I choose appropriate material using language that I know?

Make sure that everything you write is relevant to the question. Select ideas that allow you to use the language you know. Choose German words that you know to be correct.

① Practise using language that you know. Fill in 🖉 the gaps in these sentences by writing a suitable word or words that you know to be correct.

a Meine Stadt hat eine .... und einen ....

b Ich .... die Geschäfte und Restaurants.

c Es gibt kein .... in meiner Stadt.

d Die Sehenswürdigkeiten sind ....

e Ich .... in die Stadt, weil es keine Busse gibt.

f Man sollte die .... verbessern.

g Letzte Woche habe ich .... im Sportzentrum ....

h Ich bin auch ins .... gegangen.

② On the left are some difficult ideas that you might not know how to write in German. Draw lines 🖉 to match each idea with a simpler German phrase that is close in meaning.

A leisure facilities	**a** öffentliche Verkehrsmittel
B park and ride buses	**b** Geschäfte
C historic buildings and monuments	**c** ein Sportzentrum und ein Kino
D cars and lorries	**d** Verkehr
E boutiques	**e** Sehenswürdigkeiten

③ Write down 🖉 in English three things about your town or village. Then think of how you can express each idea using German that you know. An example has been done to get you started.

English idea	Using German that I know
I can't imagine anything worse than living in a big city.	Ich möchte nicht in einer Großstadt wohnen.

2 How do I organise my writing?

It's important to place your ideas in an order that makes sense. Using paragraphs can help with this. Keep all the ideas addressing the same bullet point together.

1 Here is the sample answer that you saw on page 42 again. Draw ✏ vertical lines to show where you could start new paragraphs.

> Ich wohne in einer kleinen Stadt in Südwestengland. Ich mag meine Stadt, weil es viel zu tun gibt. Wir haben ein Kino, ein Schwimmbad und einen Park. Es wird ein Fußballstadion geben. Aber in meiner Stadt gibt es auch viel Verkehr und viel Lärm. Das ist ein großer Nachteil. Letzten Samstag bin ich mit meinem Bruder in die Stadtmitte gegangen. Ich habe Kleidung gekauft und wir haben in einem China-Restaurant gegessen. Mein Bruder hat nichts gekauft. Ich möchte später in Exeter wohnen, denn es gibt dort eine gute Universität. Ich will nicht auf dem Land wohnen.

2 Look at the following pairs of sentences. Tick ✓ the pairs that go well together.

a Ich wohne auf dem Land. Es gibt nicht viel Lärm.

b Meine Stadt ist schön. Ich möchte Urlaub in Schottland machen.

c Es wird ein Stadion geben. Ich möchte die Fußballspiele dort sehen.

d Ich habe Kleidung gekauft. Das Essen hat besonders gut geschmeckt.

e Ich bin mit dem Bus gefahren. Die Fahrt war schnell.

3 Draw lines ✏ to link pairs of sentences that go well together.

A Ich wohne auf einem ruhigen Bauernhof.

B Wir haben viel Verkehr in der Stadt.

C Es gibt viel für Jugendliche zu tun.

D Man sollte die öffentlichen Verkehrsmittel verbessern.

E Ich möchte das neue Museum besuchen.

a Es gibt viel Lärm.

b Es gibt nicht genug Busse.

c Die Stadt hat ein Sportzentrum, ein Kino und ein Stadion.

d Das wird interessant sein.

e Er ist in der Nähe von einem kleinen Dorf.

4 On paper, write ✏ your own sentences to follow on from each sentence below.

a Ich mag die Großstadt am liebsten.

b Es gibt keine Buslinie in meinem Dorf.

c Wir haben ein schönes Restaurant.

d Ich werde später auf dem Land wohnen.

3 How do I use conjunctions appropriately?

Use conjunctions to link your ideas together. Be careful because different conjunctions are followed by different word order. Some common examples are listed in the table.

conjunction	meaning	word order
und	and	+ normal word order
aber	but	
denn	because	
weil	because	+ verb to end of clause
also	therefore	+ inversion (verb comes next)
dann	then / next	
auch	also	normally goes after the verb

1 Practise choosing suitable conjunctions. Circle Ⓐ the correct conjunction in each sentence.

Think about how the two parts of the sentence fit together. If the second part:
- contrasts with the first part, use *aber*
- mentions a similar thing, use *und*
- gives a reason, use *denn* or *weil*
- gives a consequence, use *also*.

a Ich wohne gern in meiner Stadt, **aber / denn** man kann viel tun.

b Mein Freund fährt jeden Tag in die Stadt **aber / und** geht gern einkaufen.

c Wir haben ein Kino, **aber / auch** kein Schwimmbad.

d Ich wohne gern hier, **denn / weil** es nicht viel Lärm gibt.

e Wir kaufen Geschenke, **weil / dann** gehen wir ins Restaurant.

2 Complete ✏ these sentences by inserting a suitable conjunction from the table at the top of the page.

Remember that you need a comma before most conjunctions, but there is no comma before *und*.

a Mein Dorf ist sehr schön .... es gibt nicht viel Verkehr.

b Es gibt viel für Jugendliche zu tun, ... alles ist teuer.

c Ich möchte Kleidung kaufen, ... gehe ich in die Stadt.

d Wir essen im italienischen Restaurant, ... das Essen dort gut schmeckt.

e Man sollte die öffentlichen Verkehrsmittel verbessern, ... es gibt zu viele Autos in der Stadtmitte.

3 Rewrite ✏ the following paragraph on paper, putting in appropriate conjunctions. Don't forget to change the word order where necessary!

There is more than one correct answer here. Think about which sentences go well together and could be joined by conjunctions.

Ich wohne auf einem Bauernhof. Es ist total ruhig. Es gibt keine Buslinie bis in die Stadt. Man sollte die öffentlichen Verkehrsmittel verbessern. Früher habe ich in einer großen Stadt gewohnt. Das war gut. Es gab viele Geschäfte und Cafés in der Nähe. Es gab zu viel Verkehr. Das war ein großer Nachteil für mich. In Zukunft möchte ich auf dem Land wohnen. Ich kann mit meinem Hund spazieren gehen. Meine Schwester will in der Hauptstadt wohnen. Es ist dort nie langweilig.

Sample response

Look at this new exam-style writing task and the student's answer below.

Exam-style question

Dein Freund Oskar aus Österreich hat dich nach deinen Ferien gefragt. Du bist jetzt im Urlaub und schreibst Oskar eine E-Mail.

Schreib:

- wo du im Urlaub bist
- was du dort gemacht hast
- warum du dein Urlaubsziel magst oder nicht magst
- wo du nächstes Jahr Urlaub machen möchtest.

Du musst ungefähr **90** Wörter auf **Deutsch** schreiben. Schreib etwas über alle Punkte der Aufgabe.

(16 marks)

Ich mache mit meiner Familie Urlaub im Schwarzwald*. Die Sonne scheint jeden Tag, aber es ist ziemlich kalt. Gestern hat es geschneit! Ich bin gern hier, weil ich sportlich bin und es Tennisplätze auf dem Campingplatz gibt. Man kann auch Fahrräder mieten**. Es gibt eine Buslinie, also brauchen wir kein Auto. Morgen fahren wir nach Freiburg und gehen einkaufen. Dann wollen wir ein Picknick machen und vielleicht ein Museum besuchen. Ich mag den Schwarzwald, aber nächstes Jahr möchte ich lieber in Spanien Urlaub machen, weil das Wetter dort wärmer ist.

* der Schwarzwald = the Black Forest
** mieten = to hire

1 Draw ✏ vertical lines in this student's answer to show where you could start new paragraphs.

Remember to keep sentences addressing each individual bullet point together in the same paragraph.

2 a Circle Ⓐ the conjunctions in the student's answer.

b Then translate ✏ into English each phrase that begins with a conjunction.

....
....
....
....
....
....

3 a The student missed out one bullet point from the exam-style question. Which one is it? ✏
....

b On paper, write ✏ a sentence or two in German to cover this point.

Your turn!

You are now going to plan and write your response to this exam-style task.

Exam-style question

Deine Freundin Melina aus der Schweiz hat dich nach deinem Wohnort gefragt. Du schreibst Melina eine E-Mail über deine Stadt.

Schreib:

- warum du deine Stadt magst oder nicht magst
- was du nächste Woche in deiner Stadt machen wirst
- etwas über eine andere Stadt, die du besucht hast
- deine ideale Stadt.

Du musst ungefähr **90** Wörter auf **Deutsch** schreiben. Schreib etwas über alle Punkte der Aufgabe.

(16 marks)

1 Plan your answer. Think of two things to write about each bullet point. Write ✏️ key words and phrases in German in the boxes.

Bullet point	Idea 1	Idea 2
warum du deine Stadt magst oder nicht magst		
was du nächste Woche in deiner Stadt machen wirst		
etwas über eine andere Stadt, die du besucht hast		
deine ideale Stadt		

2 Now write ✏️ your response to the above exam-style question on paper, using the checklist to help you.

Checklist	✓		✓
In my answer do I ...			
make sure what I write is relevant to the question?		keep ideas addressing the same bullet point together?	
use language that I know is correct, simplifying ideas if necessary?		choose the correct conjunctions to link ideas?	
start a new paragraph for a new idea?		check my word order?	

Review your skills

Check up

Review your response to the exam-style question on page 47. Tick ✓ the column to show how well you think you have done each of the following.

	Not quite ✓	Nearly there ✓	Got it! ✓
chosen appropriate material using language that you know	☐	☐	☐
organised writing	☐	☐	☐
used conjunctions appropriately	☐	☐	☐

Need more practice?

On paper, plan and write 🖉 your response to the task below.

Exam-style question

Dein Freund Emil aus Deutschland hat dich nach deinen Ferien gefragt. Du bist jetzt im Urlaub und schreibst Emil eine E-Mail.

Schreib:

- was du am Urlaubsort machst
- wie du gefahren bist
- etwas über deine Pläne für die nächsten Tage
- was besser ist – der Urlaubsort oder deine Stadt.

Du musst ungefähr **90** Wörter auf **Deutsch** schreiben. Schreib etwas über alle Punkte der Aufgabe.

(16 marks)

How confident do you feel about each of these **skills?** Colour 🖉 in the bars.

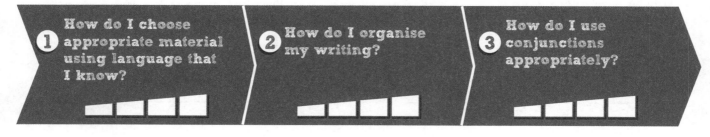

1 How do I choose appropriate material using language that I know?

2 How do I organise my writing?

3 How do I use conjunctions appropriately?

Get started

⑦ Giving and explaining your opinions

This unit will help you learn how to give and explain your opinions effectively. The skills you will build are to:

- make your opinions relevant to the topic
- add detail to your opinions
- justify your opinions.

In the exam, you will be asked to tackle a writing task like the one below. This unit will prepare you to write your own responses to these questions.

The three key questions in the **skills boosts** will help you give and explain your opinions.

① How do I make my opinions relevant to the topic?   **②** How do I add detail to my opinions?   **③** How do I justify my opinions?

Look at the sample student response to this task on the next page.

> Ich möchte vielleicht in einem Krankenhaus arbeiten. Als Kind wollte ich Ärztin werden, aber jetzt möchte ich lieber Krankenschwester werden. Dieser Job gefällt mir, weil ich geduldig bin und ich Menschen helfen möchte. Ich werde viele Stunden arbeiten, aber es wird nie langweilig sein. Ich habe schon als Freiwillige in einem Altenheim gearbeitet und das war interessant. Ich habe auch eine Woche in einem Restaurant gearbeitet, aber das hat mir keinen Spaß gemacht. In Zukunft möchte ich in der Schweiz arbeiten, weil ich gern Fremdsprachen spreche und ich gute Noten in Deutsch bekomme.

1 a First, make sure you understand the German. Tick ✓ the three things that are mentioned in the student's response.

preferred career	☐	another family member's career	☐	a past visit to Switzerland	☐
personal qualities	☐	work experience in a shop	☐	reason for wanting to work in Switzerland	☐

b Tick ✓ the four statements that are true according to the student's answer above.

Jetzt möchte ich Ärztin werden.	☐	Ich habe Arbeitserfahrung.	☐
Ich bin geduldig.	☐	Die Arbeit im Restaurant war gut.	☐
Die Arbeitszeiten werden oft lang sein.	☐	Ich möchte im Ausland arbeiten.	☐
Der Job als Krankenschwester wird vielleicht langweilig sein.	☐	Meine Deutschkenntnisse sind schlecht.	☐

2 a The student gives several opinions about her choice of job and her work experience. Write 🖉 answers in German to the following questions. You don't always have to write in sentences.

i Warum gefällt dir der Job als Krankenschwester?

....

ii Wie wirst du den Job finden?

....

iii Wie war deine Arbeitserfahrung im Altenheim?

....

iv Wie hast du deinen Job im Restaurant gefunden?

....

b The student has used different tenses to give her opinions. For each answer in **a**, write 🖉 above each verb which tense you have used.

> Giving simple opinions in different tenses:
> Present: *Das ist [toll]*.
> Past: *Das war [furchtbar]*.
> Future: *Das wird [interessant] sein.*

1 How do I make my opinions relevant to the topic?

Using adjectives is a great way of giving your opinion. Make sure that your adjectives are appropriate to the topic. Use a range of adjectives to make your writing more interesting.

1 Look at the opinions below. Fill in 🖉 the missing letters to form adjectives.

a Biologie ist i__ter__s__ant.

b Die Hausaufgaben werden s__hw__eri__ sein.

c Ich finde Horrorgeschichten s__hr__c__li__h.

d Die Eintrittskarten waren zu t__u____.

e Der Film war u__ter__alt__a__.

f Ich finde Svenja sehr k__e__t__v.

g Kommunikation ist für mich total w__c__t__g.

h Ein guter Freund muss s__mp__th__s__h sein.

2 You can use appropriate adjectives to give reasons for what you do. Circle Ⓐ the adjective (or adverb) that makes more sense in each sentence.

a Ich mag die Wohnung, weil sie **modern / jung** ist.

b Ich esse ein Spiegelei, weil es **billig / köstlich** schmeckt.

c Ich rufe vom Handy an, weil es so **schrecklich / praktisch** ist.

d Wir haben uns im Restaurant beschwert, weil das Essen **unbequem / ekelhaft** war.

e Ich kaufe dieses T-Shirt, weil es **salzig / preiswert** ist.

f Wir werden mit dem Bus fahren, weil es **umweltfreundlich / wichtig** ist.

3 The use of *gut* in each of these sentences isn't very interesting. Write 🖉 a more appropriate adjective each time. Then translate 🖉 each sentence into English.

a Die Zimmer in unserem Hotel waren ~~gut~~ ....

....

b Ich werde Achterbahn fahren, denn das finde ich immer ~~gut~~ ....

....

c Wir lernen Spanisch, weil wir Fremdsprachen ~~gut~~ .... finden.

....

d Ich möchte Elektriker werden, weil das Gehalt ~~gut~~ .... ist.

....

4 You can also give your opinion by adding an adjective before the noun. Write 🖉 an appropriate adjective from the box in each gap. The endings are done for you.

a Das war ein .... es. Abendessen.

b Das sind .... e. Hausaufgaben.

c Sie ist eine .... e. Athletin.

d Das ist eine .... e. Sendung.

e Wir haben in einem .... en. Hotel übernachtet.

f Wir hatten ein .... es. Zimmer mit Dusche und Fernseher.

begabt
bequem
lecker
schwierig
toll
unterhaltsam

② How do I add detail to my opinions?

Use opportunities to develop your opinions by adding an example or explanation.

Use a range of ways of expressing your opinions. For example:
ich mag [+ noun] – I like …   [noun] *gefällt mir* – I like …
ich [+ verb] *gern* – I like …ing   [noun] *macht Spaß* – … is fun
mein(e) Lieblings… ist … – my favourite … is …

① Look at these pairs of sentences. Tick ⊘ the ones where the second sentence develops the opinion in the first sentence.

a Die Wohnung gefällt mir. Sie hat sechs Zimmer.

b Ich mag das Haus. Das Essen hat gut geschmeckt.

c Ich mag meine Freunde. Ich habe ein gutes Schulzeugnis bekommen.

d Der Braten schmeckt mir nicht. Er ist zu salzig.

e Mein Lieblingssport ist Turnen. Ich freue mich auf Weihnachten.

f Ich höre gern Musik. Manchmal singe ich mit.

② Draw lines ✐ to match each opinion on the left with the sentence on the right that gives more detail about the opinion.

Remember that German has three different words for 'it': *er* if the noun is masculine, *sie* if the noun is feminine, *es* if the noun is neuter.

A Der Schultag ist lang.	**a** Sie ist unbequem.
B Mathe macht mir Spaß.	**b** Ich hatte gestern sechs Stunden.
C Ich mag die Schuluniform nicht.	**c** Er ist immer eifersüchtig auf mich.
D Ich bin sportlich.	**d** Er ist realistisch.
E Ich empfehle den Film.	**e** Die Lehrerin ist lustig.
F Ich verstehe mich gut mit meiner Schwester.	**f** Meine Eltern waren nicht streng.
G Ich hatte eine schöne Kindheit.	**g** Sie hat immer Zeit für mich.
H Markus und ich sind keine guten Freunde.	**h** Ich trainiere dreimal pro Woche.

Use qualifiers to make your opinions more specific. As well as the common ones such as *sehr, zu, ziemlich* you could try these:
vielleicht – maybe   *Das wird **vielleicht** Spaß machen.*
total – completely   *Das war **total** lecker.*
besonders – specially   *Das ist **besonders** interessant.*

③ How do I justify my opinions?

Look out for the word *warum* (why) in writing tasks. This tells you that you need to give a reason for your opinions. If you use a word for 'because' to introduce your reasons, be careful with the word order: *weil* sends the verb to the end, but *denn* doesn't.

① Look at these sentences, which give an opinion and a reason. The word order is incorrect. Circle Ⓐ the verb and draw 🖉 an arrow to show where it should be in the sentence.

a Kunst ist mein Lieblingsfach, denn die Hausaufgaben interessant sind.

b Ich mag Mathe nicht, weil ich bekomme schlechte Noten.

c Der Film war nicht gut, weil die Schauspieler waren unrealistisch.

d Mein Lieblingssport ist Skifahren, denn bin ich gern in den Bergen.

e Ich empfehle das Festival, weil die Musik ist immer lebhaft.

② Complete 🖉 these opinions with reasons by writing a suitable verb in each gap.

a Die Schweiz ist ein beliebtes Reiseziel, weil es Berge ....

b Meine Lieblingsjahreszeit ist der Sommer, denn es .... oft sonnig.

c Wir wollen Skiurlaub machen, weil wir aktiv ....

d Ich möchte Pilotin werden, denn ich .... um die Welt reisen.

e Ich mache meinen Job gern, weil ich kreativ ....

③ Complete 🖉 the following sentences by writing why you would like or not like to do each job. Cross out the word *nicht* if appropriate, and circle Ⓐ the correct form of the job word for you. You can use the ideas in the box or your own ideas.

ich bin sportlich   ich finde aktuelle Themen interessant   ich helfe gern Menschen

ich interessiere mich für das Theater   ich mag Tiere

a Ich möchte (nicht) Journalist/Journalistin werden, weil ....

....

b Ich möchte (nicht) Tierarzt/Tierärztin werden, denn ....

....

c Ich möchte (nicht) Krankenpfleger/Krankenschwester werden, weil ....

....

d Ich möchte (nicht) Assistent/Assistentin an einer Skischule werden, denn ....

....

e Ich möchte (nicht) Schauspieler/Schauspielerin werden, weil ....

....

④ Now think of three more jobs. On paper, write 🖉 sentences like those in ③ to say why you would or would not like to do each job.

Sample response

To give and explain opinions effectively, you need to:

- make your opinions relevant to the topic
- add detail to your opinions
- justify your opinions.

Look at this new exam-style writing task and the student's response below.

Exam-style question

Deine deutsche Freundin Katharina kann dir vielleicht helfen, einen Ferienjob zu finden. Du schreibst Katharina eine E-Mail.

Schreib:

- etwas über deine Charaktereigenschaften
- etwas über deine Arbeitserfahrung
- wo du in den Ferien arbeiten möchtest und warum
- etwas über deine Berufspläne.

Du musst ungefähr **90** Wörter auf **Deutsch** schreiben. Schreib etwas über alle Punkte der Aufgabe.

(16 marks)

Ich bin sehr fleißig in der Schule und bekomme gute Noten. Ich bin pünktlich und zuverlässig. Seit zwei Jahren bin ich Mitglied im Schulorchester. Ich mache das gern, weil ich musikalisch bin. Ich habe schon in einer Bibliothek gearbeitet. Das war gut, denn ich liebe Bücher. Ich möchte dieses Jahr in Deutschland arbeiten. Das wird interessant sein, weil ich Französisch und Deutsch lerne und ich meine Sprachkenntnisse verbessern will. Vielleicht kann ich einen Job in einem Hotel bekommen. Wenn ich älter bin, möchte ich bei einer internationalen Firma arbeiten.

(1) Draw ✏ vertical lines in this student's answer to show where the answer to each bullet point begins.

(2) There are three opinions with reasons in the student's answer. Summarise ✏ them in English in the table.

Opinion	Reason

Your turn!

You are now going to plan and write your response to this exam-style task.

Exam-style question

Deine österreichische Freundin Alina hat dich nach deinen Berufsplänen gefragt. Du schreibst Alina eine E-Mail.

Schreib:

- etwas über deine Arbeitserfahrung
- warum du diesen Job gern oder nicht gern gemacht hast
- etwas über deinen Traumberuf
- etwas über einen Job, den du **nicht** machen möchtest.

Du musst ungefähr **90** Wörter auf **Deutsch** schreiben. Schreib etwas über alle Punkte der Aufgabe.

(16 marks)

1 Plan your answer. Think of two things to write about each bullet point. Write 🖊 key words and phrases in German in the boxes.

Bullet point	Idea 1	Idea 2
etwas über deine Arbeitserfahrung		
warum du diesen Job gern oder nicht gern gemacht hast		
etwas über deinen Traumberuf		
etwas über einen Job, den du **nicht** machen möchtest		

2 Now write 🖊 your response to the above exam-style question on paper, using the checklist to help you.

Checklist	✓		✓
In my answer do I ...		express my opinions in different ways?	
choose adjectives appropriate to the topic?		use qualifiers correctly?	
use a variety of adjectives?		use *weil* or *denn* to give reasons?	
add detail by giving an example or explanation?		use the correct word order with *weil* and *denn*?	

Unit 7 Giving and explaining your opinions   **55**

Review your skills

Check up

Review your response to the exam-style question on page 55. Tick ✓ the column to show how well you think you have done each of the following.

	Not quite ✓	Nearly there ✓	Got it! ✓
made opinions relevant to the topic	☐	☐	☐
added detail to opinions	☐	☐	☐
justified opinions	☐	☐	☐

Need more practice?

On paper, plan and write your response to the task below.

Exam-style question

Deine deutsche Freundin kann dir vielleicht helfen, einen Ferienjob zu finden. Du schreibst ihr eine E-Mail.

Schreib:

* etwas über deine Sprachkenntnisse
* wie du deine Sprachkenntnisse benutzt hast
* wo du in den Ferien arbeiten möchtest und warum
* etwas über deine Berufspläne.

Du musst ungefähr **90** Wörter auf **Deutsch** schreiben. Schreib etwas über alle Punkte der Aufgabe.

(16 marks)

How confident do you feel about each of these **skills?** Colour ✏ in the bars.

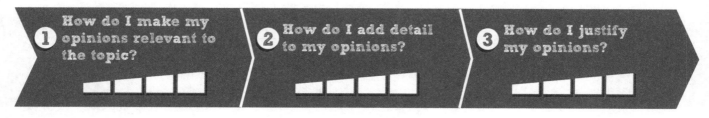

1 How do I make my opinions relevant to the topic?

2 How do I add detail to my opinions?

3 How do I justify my opinions?

Translating from English into German

This unit will help you learn how to translate into German successfully. The skills you will build are to:

- avoid translating too literally
- translate precisely without paraphrasing
- avoid the pitfalls of translation.

In the exam, you will be asked to tackle a translation task like the one below. This unit will prepare you to write your own responses to these questions.

Exam-style question

Translate the following sentences into **German**.

Our school is quite large.

We are not allowed to eat in the classrooms.

Biology is my favourite subject because it is easy.

Last week I didn't do any homework.

I am looking forward to the school trip.

(10 marks)

The three key questions in the **skills boosts** will help you translate into German successfully.

1 How do I avoid translating too literally?

2 How do I translate precisely without paraphrasing?

3 How do I avoid the pitfalls of translation?

Look at the sample student response on the next page.

Exam-style question

Translate the following sentences into **German**.

Our school is quite large.

Unsere Schule ist ziemlich groß.

We are not allowed to eat in the classrooms.

Wir dürfen nicht in den Klassenzimmern essen.

Biology is my favourite subject because it is easy.

Mein Lieblingsfach ist Biologie, weil es einfach ist.

Last week I didn't do any homework.

Letzte Woche habe ich keine Hausaufgaben gemacht.

I am looking forward to the school trip.

Ich freue mich auf die Klassenfahrt.

(10 marks)

1. Look at the student's answer above and write down ✐ one example of each of the following.

   a two English words translated by a single German word ....

   ....

   b a verb referring to the past ....

   c a negative that isn't *nicht* ....

   d a verb referring to the future ....

   e a modal verb followed by an infinitive

   ....

   > Modal verbs are verbs like *müssen* and *dürfen*. They are usually used with the infinitive of a different verb. For example: *Wir **müssen** nach Hause **gehen**.*

   f a noun in the dative plural ....

   g subordinate word order (verb to end of clause) ....

2. Look again at the student's answer above and answer ✐ these questions in English.

   a In the first sentence, why does *unsere* end in *-e*?

   ....

   b In the first sentence, why does the adjective *groß* not have an ending?

   ....

   c In the third sentence, why is it *mein*, not *meine*?

   ....

   d In the third sentence, why is the word for 'it' *es*?

   ....

   e Is the German for 'look forward to' a separable verb or a reflexive verb? How can you tell?

   > Here are examples of these two types of verb:
   > Separable verb: *fernsehen* (to watch TV) – *ich sehe fern*
   > Reflexive verb: *sich setzen* (to sit down) – *ich setze mich*

   ....

① How do I avoid translating too literally?

Don't automatically translate one English word with one German word. Take care with word order, too.

① Draw lines 🖉 to match each sentence with what you need to watch out for when translating it into German.

A Every day I watch the news.	**a** Two words will be translated by a single German word.
B I like meeting friends.	**b** An English verb will be translated by the German adverb *gern*.
C We read love stories.	**c** A change in word order so the verb is the second idea.
D I like cartoons because they are entertaining.	**d** A change in word order – the verb will go to the end of the clause.

② Translate 🖉 the sentences in ① into German. Some of the words you need are given in the box.

a ....

b ....

c ....

d ....
....

> lesen
> mag
> Nachrichten
> treffe
> unterhaltsam
> Zeichentrickfilme

③ Look at these sentences. Below each sentence, write 🖉 in English why a literal, word-for-word translation won't work.

a We like playing handball.

....

> How will you translate 'like playing'?

b I went to a festival.

....

> Think about how the perfect tense works in German.

c At home I watch videos.

....

> Think about word order.

d I buy magazines because they are interesting.

....

> What is special about the German for 'because'?

④ Translate 🖉 the sentences in ③ into German. Some of the words you need are given in the box.

a ....

b ....

c ....

d ....

> Festival
> Handball
> interessant
> Videos
> Zeitschriften
> zu Hause

② How do I translate precisely without paraphrasing?

Make sure that you include all essential information and don't change the meaning of the English sentence.

① Look at the translations of the following English sentences. Tick ✓ the translations that are correct and cross ✗ those that don't mean quite the same thing.

a I get on well with Veronika.

> Veronika ist meine beste Freundin. ☐

b Uwe is nice and fairly intelligent.

> Uwe ist nett und ziemlich intelligent. ☐

c Kai is always jealous of me.

> Kai ist immer eifersüchtig auf mich. ☐

d I spend a lot of time with grandma.

> Meine Oma hat Zeit für mich. ☐

e It is not my computer.

> Ich darf den Computer nicht benutzen. ☐

f Last year we went to Bonn.

> Letztes Jahr sind wir nach Bonn gefahren. ☐

② Look at the following alternative translations. Tick ✓ the correct translation each time.

a Finya gets on my nerves.

> Finya geht mir auf die Nerven. ☐
>
> Ich streite mich mit Finya. ☐

b She's going out with my brother.

> Sie versteht sich gut mit meinem Bruder. ☐
>
> Sie geht mit meinem Bruder aus. ☐

c We had fun in Munich.

> Wir haben in München Spaß gehabt. ☐
>
> Wir haben München interessant gefunden. ☐

d I will get on with her better.

> Ich werde mich besser mit ihr verstehen. ☐
>
> Ich werde sie besser kennenlernen. ☐

③ On paper, rewrite ✎ these German sentences so that they translate the English more accurately.

a He gets on fairly well with his dad.

> Er versteht sich gut mit seinem Vater.

b I spend too much time in front of the TV.

> Ich verbringe Zeit vor dem Fernseher.

c A good friend must have lots of patience.

> Ein guter Freund hat viel Geduld.

d Her favourite hobby is swimming.

> Ihr Hobby ist Schwimmen.

e Paula has a new boyfriend called Max.

> Paula hat einen Freund und er heißt Max.

f He is not allowed to go out at the moment.

> Im Moment darf er nicht ins Kino gehen.

3 How do I avoid the pitfalls of translation?

Watch out for these two pitfalls of translation:

- 'false friends' – German words that look similar to English words but have a different meaning
- English words that have more than one German translation – always check the context.

1 These German words look similar to English words but actually mean something different. Find the correct English translation of each word in the box and write ✏ it next to the German.

a Informatik .... **f** das Kind ....

b das Handy .... **g** der Flur ....

c wandern .... **h** das Mobbing ....

d sympathisch .... **i** der See ....

e nervig .... **j** aktuell ....

| annoying | child | mobile phone | bullying | lake |
| ICT | nice | current (up to date) | hall, corridor | to hike |

2 Translate ✏ the following sentences into German, using the words from **1**.

a That was really annoying. ....

b I am not a child. ....

Remember to use *kein* here (not *nicht ein*, as this is incorrect German).

c A mobile phone is important.

....

d Bullying is a problem. ....

e The lake was big. ....

f On Tuesday we have ICT. ....

g My stepdad is nice. ....

h That is not current. ....

i The cat is sitting in the corridor. ....

j We like hiking. ....

3 Circle Ⓐ the German word that correctly translates the bold word in each English sentence.

a My grandma is **nice** to me.   Meine Oma ist **nett / schön** zu mir.

b I'm going by train **this time**.   Ich fahre **diese Zeit / dieses Mal** mit dem Zug.

c The journey **took** an hour.   Die Reise hat eine Stunde **genommen / gedauert**.

d My **room** is too small.   Mein **Platz / Zimmer** ist zu klein.

e The days **are getting** longer.   Die Tage **werden / bekommen** länger.

f How do we **get** to the city?   Wie **kommen / bekommen** wir zur Stadt?

g I can't **stand** my stepsister.   Ich kann meine Stiefschwester nicht **leiden / stehen**.

Sample response

When you translate, you should:

- avoid translating too literally
- translate precisely without paraphrasing
- avoid the pitfalls of translation.

Look at this exam-style translation task and the student's answer. Each sentence in the student's answer contains one error.

Exam-style question

Translate the following sentences into **German**.

In the evening we don't eat much.

Am Abend wir essen nicht viel.

My room is on the first floor.

Mein Raum ist im ersten Stock.

I like my flat because it's modern.

Ich mag meine Wohnung, weil sie ist modern.

I often play tennis at the weekend.

Ich spiele Tennis am Wochenende.

My sister uses social networks.

Meine Schwester findet soziale Netzwerke wichtig.

(10 marks)

① Write ✐ in English next to each sentence what needs correcting.

② Write ✐ a correct German translation of each sentence in the exam-style question above.

③ On paper, translate ✐ the following sentences into German, watching out for similar pitfalls.

- a In the afternoon we do sport.
- b This year I will train a lot.
- c I often get tired.
- d My favourite sport is athletics because it is healthy.
- e I listen to music when I am at home.
- f We spend six hours a day in school.
- g Last year I had a problem with bullying.

Your turn!

You are now going to plan and write your response to this exam-style task.

Exam-style question

Translate the following sentences into **German**.

I go by bus because it is practical.

Trains are a lot more environmentally friendly than cars.

Last year we stayed on a campsite.

The soup was nice but the cutlet was cold.

I'm also looking for a present.

Don't translate 'more environmentally friendly' word for word. To form comparative adjectives in German, you add –er to the end of the adjective.

(10 marks)

1 Plan your answer. Write ✐ in English two possible difficulties when translating each sentence.

Bullet point	Difficulty 1	Difficulty 2
I go by bus because it is practical.		
Trains are a lot more environmentally friendly than cars.		
Last year we stayed on a campsite.		
The soup was nice but the cutlet was cold.		
I am also looking for a present.		

2 Now write ✐ your response to the above exam-style question on paper, using the checklist to help you.

Checklist	✓		✓
In my answer do I ...		avoid changing the meaning?	
avoid simply translating word for word?		watch out for 'false friends'?	
make sure my word order is correct?		make sure I have used the correct German words for the context?	
ensure I've included essential information?			

Review your skills

Check up

Review your response to the exam-style question on page 63. Tick ✓ the column to show how well you think you have done each of the following.

	Not quite ✓	Nearly there ✓	Got it! ✓
avoided translating too literally	☐	☐	☐
translated precisely without paraphrasing	☐	☐	☐
avoided the pitfalls of translation	☐	☐	☐

Need more practice?

Write ✏ your response to the task below. Plan first on paper.

Exam-style question

Translate the following sentences into **German**.

In the summer it is often too hot.

....

We like spending a lot of time with friends.

....

Last year they went by train.

....

....

The campsite was quiet because there were no cars.

....

....

I can get to Germany.

....

(10 marks)

How confident do you feel about each of these **skills**? Colour ✏ in the bars.

1 How do I avoid translating too literally?

2 How do I translate precisely without paraphrasing?

3 How do I avoid the pitfalls of translation?

⑨ Using complex language effectively

This unit will help you learn how to use complex language effectively. The skills you will build are to:

- broaden your range of vocabulary
- broaden your range of grammatical structures
- use idiom effectively.

In the Higher exam, you will be asked to tackle a writing task like the one below. This unit will prepare you to write your own responses to these questions.

Exam-style question

Deine deutsche Freundin Melina hat dich nach Festivals und Events gefragt. Du schreibst Melina eine E-Mail.

- Was ist dein Lieblingsevent und warum?

- Vergleiche ein Event, das du besucht oder gesehen hast, und ein Event, das du in Zukunft besuchen möchtest.

Du musst ungefähr **150** Wörter auf **Deutsch** schreiben. Schreib etwas über **beide** Punkte der Aufgabe.

(32 marks)

The three key questions in the **skills boosts** will help you use complex language effectively.

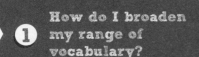

1 How do I broaden my range of vocabulary?

2 How do I broaden my range of grammatical structures?

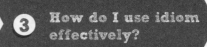

3 How do I use idiom effectively?

Look at the sample student response on the next page.

> Mein Lieblingsevent ist die Fußball-Weltmeisterschaft. Das ist ein Turnier für Nationalmannschaften. Alle vier Jahre kämpfen mehr als dreißig Mannschaften im Turnier. 2014 hat die Endrunde in Brasilien stattgefunden und Deutschland hat gewonnen. Ich finde die Weltmeisterschaft total spannend. Ich spiele gern Fußball und bin in der Schulmannschaft. Meine Freundinnen und Freunde sind auch Fußballfans. Wir sprechen jeden Tag über Fußball und gehen oft zum Stadion. Ich habe das Finale der Weltmeisterschaft im Fernsehen gesehen, denn ich konnte nicht nach Brasilien fliegen. Der Flug und die Eintrittskarten waren viel zu teuer. Aber das Spiel im Fernsehen war auch super. Ich habe geschrien, als Deutschland gewonnen hat. Obwohl ich Fußballfan bin, interessiere ich mich auch für andere Sportarten, und ich möchte in Zukunft die Olympischen Winterspiele besuchen. Sie finden im Februar statt. Das wird kalt, aber ganz toll sein. Ich lerne seit zwei Jahren Skifahren und mache nächsten Februar einen Skiurlaub.

1 **a** First, make sure you understand the German. Tick ✓ the three things that are mentioned in the student's response.

how often the World Cup takes place ☐	when the next World Cup will take place ☐	watching the World Cup on TV ☐
the winner of the 2014 World Cup ☐	where the next World Cup will take place ☐	seeing the Summer Olympics ☐

b Tick ✓ the three statements that are true according to the student's answer above.

Ich finde die Fußball-Weltmeisterschaft zu laut. ☐

Die Fußball-Weltmeisterschaft findet alle vier Jahre statt. ☐

Deutschland gewinnt immer die Fußball-Weltmeisterschaft. ☐

Meine Freunde interessieren sich für Fußball. ☐

Der Flug nach Brasilien war teuer. ☐

Im Februar will ich Brasilien besuchen. ☐

2 Find the German for these English words and phrases in the student's answer and write ✎ it next to the English. All the words are to do with sports and sporting events.

a the world championships .... ☐

b in the tournament .... ☐

c to compete .... ☐

d took place .... ☐

e in the school team .... ☐

f the final .... ☐

g the tickets .... ☐

h won .... ☐

i types of sport .... ☐

j the Winter Olympics .... ☐

3 Tick ✓ all the words in **2** that you could use to talk about your own sporting interests and then learn them.

1 How do I broaden my range of vocabulary?

Try to avoid repeating common words and to be adventurous in your choice of vocabulary – while also taking care to check that it is appropriate for the question you are answering.

1 Practise using synonyms and different ways of expressing the same idea to vary your language. Fill in 🖉 the missing letters to write these words and phrases that mean the same or similar things. (There is more than one alternative for some of them.)

- **a** teilnehmen = m_tm_ch_n
- **b** ich mag Musik = _ch h_r_ g_rn M_s_k   _ch b_n m_s_k_l_sch
- **c** das war toll = _ch h_b_ d_s w_nd_rb_r g_f_nd_n
- **d** das interessiert mich nicht = d_s _st n_chts f_r m_ch
- **e** nicht gut = f_rchtb_r   schr_ckl_ch
- **f** billig = pr_ _sw_rt   n_cht t_ _ _ _r
- **g** gut = s_p_r   t_ll   gr_ß_rt_g

2 These sentences are repetitive. Cross out ⊗ the repeated words and phrases and write in alternative phrases above them to make the language more varied and interesting.

- **a** Die Pariser Modewoche interessiert mich nicht, denn Mode interessiert mich nicht.

- **b** Das Festival war gut und die Bands waren gut. Die Eintrittskarte war billig. Das Essen war sehr billig und lecker.

- **c** Ich mag den Eurovision Song Contest, denn ich mag Musik. Mehr also 50 Länder nehmen am Contest teil. In Zukunft will ich auch teilnehmen.

3 Practise choosing vocabulary that fits the context and makes sense. Circle Ⓐ the word in each pair that makes more sense. Then, on a piece of paper, translate each sentence into English.

- **a** Mein Bruder hat mit dem Rauchen **angefangen / geholfen**, weil er etwas Neues **aufgeben / ausprobieren** wollte.
- **b** Drogen sind **billig / gefährlich** und machen **gesund / süchtig**.
- **c** Meiner Meinung nach sollte man nicht in der **Geldverschwendung / Öffentlichkeit** vapen, weil es **entspannend / unsozial** ist.
- **d** Ein Schlafplatz auf der Straße kann **gefährlich / betrunken** sein.
- **e** Ein **Zimmer / Zentrum** für Obdachlose kann bei der Arbeitssuche helfen.
- **f** Eine Arbeitsstelle ist wichtig, um eine **teure / eigene** Wohnung zu finden.

4 Choose six words from **3** that you could use in your own writing. Write down 🖉 each word and its English meaning.

Make sure you write the gender of nouns (der/die/das) and the infinitive form of verbs.

....

....

....

Unit 9 Using complex language effectively **67**

2 How do I broaden my range of grammatical structures?

More complex structures such as subordinate clauses, *um ... zu ...* clauses and modal verbs are great ways of demonstrating your command of grammar.

1 Circle Ⓐ the subordinating conjunction that makes sense in each sentence.

a Wir können alle den Müll trennen, **als / weil** das einfach ist.

b Wir haben einen Preis gewonnen, **als / obwohl** wir ein Umweltprojekt gemacht haben.

c Ich werde Obst und Gemüse kompostieren, **obwohl / wenn** ich meinen eigenen Garten habe.

> Use a range of subordinating conjunctions as well as *weil* (because), e.g.:
> *als* (when – only used when talking about the past),
> *wenn* (when/whenever),
> *obwohl* (although).

2 Write ✎ your own subordinate clause to complete each sentence. You can use the words in the box or your own ideas.

> es   ich   wir   das Licht   manchmal   anstrengend   ausschalten   gesund bleiben   war   will

a Wir sparen Energie, **wenn** ....

b Ich will eine Fahrradwoche organisieren, **weil** ....

c Das Projekt hat Spaß gemacht, **obwohl** ....

3 Practise making sentences using *um ... zu ...* Draw lines ✎ to match each sentence beginning with the correct ending.

A Man kann das Licht ausschalten,	**a** um die Vögel zu schützen.
B Man kann Nistkästen* bauen,	**b** um Projekte zu organisieren.
C Man kann Umweltsprecher werden,	**c** um Energie zu sparen.

*Nistkästen = nest boxes

4 Practise using modal verbs with the infinitive of another verb. Write ✎ your own ending to each sentence in German. Use the ideas given in English in the box or your own ideas.

> The modal verb must agree with the subject. The other verb should be in the infinitive form at the end of the clause.

> ~~have my own flat~~   listen to our favourite music   drink less alcohol
> help in a centre for homeless people   find a job

a Ich möchte   *meine eigene Wohnung haben.*

b Wir wollen ....

c Man sollte ....

....

d Man kann ....

....

e Ich muss ....

3 How do I use idiom effectively?

Well-chosen vocabulary and a varied sentence structure will help you to write German that doesn't look as if it has been translated literally from English. Learning the German word order rules will help with this. Choosing the right prepositions (words like 'in', 'to' and 'since') is important, too.

1 These sentences all use German structures that are worded differently from the way we might say things in English. Draw lines 🖉 to match each sentence beginning with the correct ending.

A Das Positive ist,	**a** oft von Armut bedroht.
B Immigranten sind	**b** weil Freunde es gemacht haben.
C Meiner Meinung nach sind	**c** dass man bei der Arbeitssuche hilft.
D Alkohol kann	**d** seit zwei Wochen keine Zigaretten mehr.
E Mein Stiefvater raucht	**e** viel Negatives mit sich bringen.
F Ich habe Drogen genommen,	**f** E-Zigaretten gefährlich.

2 Little words like prepositions are important too, as they can change the meaning. Circle Ⓐ the preposition that makes more sense in each sentence.

a Ich mache eine Umweltaktion **an / mit** meiner Klasse.

b Meiner Meinung **nach / über** sollten wir alle den Müll trennen.

c Man könnte öfter **auf / mit** dem Rad fahren.

d Wir interessieren uns sehr **auf / für** den Umweltschutz.

e Viele Tierarten sind **am / vom** Aussterben bedroht.

f Ich möchte **bei / von** einer Hilfsorganisation für Straßenkinder arbeiten.

3 Remember that word order in German is different from in English. Tick ✓ the correct version of each sentence.

a Das Oktoberfest findet jedes Jahr statt. ☐   Das Oktoberfest stattfindet jedes Jahr. ☐

b Hast du besucht das Festival? ☐   Hast du das Festival besucht? ☐

c Das Festival, das ich gesehen habe, war toll. ☐   Das Festival, das ich habe gesehen, war toll. ☐

d Mit vierzehn Jahren hat meine Freundin mit dem Rauchen angefangen. ☐   Mit vierzehn Jahren meine Freundin hat angefangen mit dem Rauchen. ☐

4 Translate these sentences into German.

a The Okoberfest takes place in September.

b In my opinion alcohol is dangerous.

....

....

Unit 9 Using complex language effectively   **69**

Sample response

Look at this new exam-style writing task and the student's response below.

Exam-style question

Deine Freundin Maya aus Österreich hat dich nach gesellschaftlichen Problemen gefragt. Du schreibst Maya eine E-Mail.

- Schreib deine Meinung zu Rauchen, Alkohol und Drogen.

- Schreib etwas über Probleme mit Alkohol und was man gegen diese Probleme machen sollte.

Du musst ungefähr **150** Wörter auf **Deutsch** schreiben. Schreib etwas über **beide** Punkte der Aufgabe.

(32 marks)

Obwohl Rauchen nicht illegal ist, ist es manchmal tödlich. Viele Leute denken, dass Rauchen cool ist, aber man kann Lungenkrebs und andere Krankheiten bekommen. Wenn man raucht, ist es sehr schwierig aufzugeben. Außerdem sind Zigaretten teuer. E-Zigaretten sind ein bisschen besser, weil sie keine Verbrennungsprodukte haben, aber sie enthalten auch Nikotin und machen süchtig. Ich finde es unsozial, wenn man in der Öffentlichkeit vapt. Meiner Meinung nach sind Alkohol und Drogen so gefährlich wie Zigaretten. Viele Menschen trinken Alkohol oder nehmen andere Drogen, weil es entspannend ist oder weil Freunde es machen. Meine Schwester Hanna hat mit sechzehn Jahren viel Alkohol getrunken und sie wurde krank. Das war nichts Cooles und ich habe das schrecklich gefunden. Glücklicherweise hat sie das aufgegeben und es geht ihr jetzt besser. Meiner Meinung nach sollte Alkohol illegal sein. Er bringt zu viel Negatives mit sich. Wenn wir keinen Alkohol trinken, leben wir länger und gesünder.

(1) First, check that you understand the German. Tick ✓ all the things that are mentioned in the student's answer.

the dangers of smoking	☐	why the writer's sister drank alcohol	☐
the pros and cons of e-cigarettes	☐	the current age of the writer's sister	☐
the high cost of alcohol	☐	different strengths of alcoholic drinks	☐
some reasons for drinking alcohol	☐		

(2) Find examples of the following in the sample answer and use three different colours to highlight 🖉 them.

a three examples of good vocabulary

b two examples of complex sentence structure

c one example of idiom (a phrase that isn't a word-for-word translation from English)

(3) Suggest four more examples of complex language that could be used in this response. On paper, write 🖉 a phrase or sentence that includes each of the following structures.

a um ... zu ... ('in order to')

b a phrase beginning with als ('when' in the past)

c a modal verb (like müssen or können) + infinitive

d a verb referring to the future (e.g. werden + infinitive)

Your turn!

You are now going to plan and write your response to this exam-style task.

Exam-style question

Dein Freund Philipp aus der Schweiz hat dich nach gesellschaftlichen Problemen gefragt. Du schreibst Philipp eine E-Mail.

• Schreib etwas über Armut und Obdachlosigkeit in deiner Stadt.

• Wie kann man Armen und Obdachlosen helfen?

Du musst ungefähr **150** Wörter auf **Deutsch** schreiben. Schreib etwas über **beide** Punkte der Aufgabe.

(32 marks)

1 Plan your answer. Think of three things to write about each bullet point. Write 🖊 key words in German in the boxes.

Bullet point	Idea 1	Idea 2	Idea 3
Schreib etwas über Armut und Obdachlosigkeit in deiner Stadt.			
Wie kann man Armen und Obdachlosen helfen?			

2 Plan how you are going to use complex language in your answer. Write 🖊 ideas for the following that fit the context of the question.

a Three ideas for good vocabulary ....

....

b Two ideas for complex sentence structure ....

....

....

c One idea for idiom (a phrase that isn't a word-for-word translation from English) ....

....

3 Now write 🖊 your response to the above exam-style question on paper. Make sure you include all your ideas for including more complex language. Use the checklist to help you.

Checklist	✓		✓
In my answer do I ...			
use a broad range of vocabulary?		use idiom effectively?	
avoid repeating common words?		avoid translating directly from English?	
use a broad range of grammatical structures, including subordinate clauses, *um ... zu ...* clauses and modal verbs?		use a range of prepositions correctly?	

Review your skills

Check up

Review your response to the exam-style question on page 71. Tick the column to show how well you think you have done each of the following.

	Not quite ⊘	Nearly there ⊘	Got it! ⊘
broadened range of vocabulary	☐	☐	☐
broadened range of grammatical structures	☐	☐	☐
used idiom effectively	☐	☐	☐

Need more practice?

On paper, plan and write 🖉 your response to the task below.

Exam-style question

Dein deutscher Freund Noah hat dich nach Umweltaktionen gefragt. Du schreibst Noah eine E-Mail.

• Schreib deine Meinung zu Umweltaktionen in der Schule.

• Wie hast du im letzten Monat der Umwelt geholfen und wie willst du in Zukunft der Umwelt helfen?

Du musst ungefähr **150** Wörter **auf Deutsch** schreiben. Schreib etwas über **beide** Punkte der Aufgabe.

(32 marks)

How confident do you feel about each of these **skills?** Colour 🖉 in the bars.

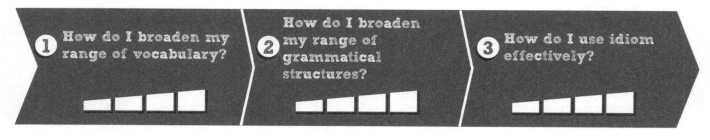

1 How do I broaden my range of vocabulary?

2 How do I broaden my range of grammatical structures?

3 How do I use idiom effectively?

Answers

Unit 1

Page 2

(1) Tick: **a**, **d**, **e**

(2) Die Schule beginnt um 08:45 Uhr. [B3] Wir haben sechs Stunden pro Tag. [B3] Mein Lieblingsfach ist Mathe. [B1] Es ist einfach und ich bekomme gute Noten. [B1] Geschichte und Erdkunde mache ich nicht gern. [B2] Im Klassenzimmer dürfen wir nicht essen und trinken. [B4] Wir müssen pünktlich sein. [B4]

(3) **a** NR **b** B3 **c** B4 **d** B2 **e** B4 **f** NR **g** B3 **h** B1

Page 3

(1) Sample answers

Lehrer/ Lehrerin	Fächer	Schülerinnen/ Schüler	Klassenzimmer	Schultag
intelligent	interessant	fleißig	groß	stressig
streng	langweilig	freundlich	klein	schwierig
lustig	einfach	lustig	modern	lang

(2) 1 klein

2 glücklich

3 freundlich

4 groß

Page 4

(1) **a** 1 <u>Das ist eine</u> Klasse.

2 <u>Das ist ein</u> Klassenzimmer.

3 <u>Es gibt</u> eine Lehrerin.

4 <u>Es gibt</u> Schülerinnen und Schüler.

b 1 britischen

2 ziemlich

3 sehe, spricht

4 lernen, Stunde

(2) Ac, Ba, Cb, Dd

Page 5

(1) **a, b**

i (✕) die S̶h̶ule   die Schule

ii (✓)

iii (✕) die Schülerinnen   die Schülerinnen

iv (✓)

v (✕) Der Lehrerin ist streng. Die Lehrerin ist streng.

vi (✕) Ich nicht mag Mathe.   Ich mag Mathe nicht.

vii (✓)

viii (✕) Wir müssen sein pünktlich. Wir müssen pünktlich sein.

(2) 1 Wir ist in einem klassenzimmer in einer britischen Schule Shule.

2 Es gibt sechs Schülerinnen und Schüler und ein Lehrerin mit langen Haaren.

3 Der Schülerinnen und Schüler findet die Stunde interessant interresant.

4 Die Lehrerin stellen eine Frage.

(3) Mein Leiblingsfach / Lieblingsfach ist Kunst, denn die Stunden sind interessant / interresant. Ich mag / Mag Chemie nicht, denn die / der Lehrer ist / sind zu streng. Der / Die Schule beginnt um 9 Uhr und endet um 4 Uhr / um 4 Uhr endet. Wir muss / müssen eine Schuluniform tragen und punktlich / pünktlich sein. Man darf / dürfen nur in der Kantine essen / isst.

Page 6

(1)

Which answer ...	A	B	How is this done? Note the German words used.
a avoids repeating common adjectives?	✓		freundlich, einfach
b uses a range of verbs?	✓		habe, singe, finde, dürfen, müssen, werden ... gehen
c joins related ideas using *und* and *aber*?	✓		freundlich, <u>aber</u> streng; denn ich singe gern <u>und</u> die Hausaufgaben sind einfach; Wir dürfen nicht schlagen <u>und</u> müssen pünktlich sein.
d avoids errors with spelling, capital letters and verb endings?		✓	Lieblingsfach, Hausaufgaben, müssen

(2) Sample answer

Ich mag meine Lehrerinnen und Lehrer, denn sie sind nicht streng. Das Essen in der Schule ist gut. Ich finde die Schulordnung unfair. Es gibt auch zu viele Hausaufgaben und sie sind schwierig. Morgen machen wir eine Klassenfahrt und das wird interessant sein.

Page 7

(1) Sample answers

Bullet point	Vocabulary
die Klassenzimmer, Labors und so weiter	fünfundzwanzig, Naturwissenschaften
deine Schulfächer	Lieblingsfach, Informatik, wichtig, mag, Biologie
Gruppen und Clubs	viele, Tennis spielen
was du in der Schule **nicht** magst	Schulordnung, streng

(2) Sample answer

Wir haben fünfundzwanzig Klassenzimmer und es gibt sechs Labors für die Naturwissenschaften. Mein Lieblingsfach ist Informatik, weil Computer sehr wichtig sind. Ich mag auch Biologie. Wir haben viele Gruppen und Clubs. Ich spiele Tennis in der Schule. Ich finde die Schulordnung zu streng.

Page 8

Sample answers

Photo-based task

1 Auf dem Foto sehe ich drei Kinder, eine Lehrerin und einen Lehrer.

2 Sie sind in einem Klassenzimmer und es gibt Tische und Stühle.

3 Die Kinder sind vielleicht sieben oder acht Jahre alt.

4 Die Kinder lernen Kunst und finden die Stunde interessant.

40-word question

Mein Lieblingsfach ist Physik, denn die Stunden sind einfach. Ich mag Geschichte nicht, weil es viele Klassenarbeiten gibt. Die Schulordnung ist fair. Wir dürfen nicht rauchen und müssen die Schuluniform tragen. Das Essen in der Schule ist schrecklich. Ich esse Brot und trinke Wasser.

Unit 2

Page 10

(1) Tick: **a**, **d**, **f**

(2) a i bin, trainiere   ii fahre, treffe   iii gehe, mag
iv sehe ... fern, kostet

b *kostet* is not in the first person singular form.

(3) a Ich fahre am Samstag in die Stadt.

b Ich trainiere einmal pro Woche (im Verein).

c Zu Hause sehe ich gern fern.

d Ich treffe Freunde.

e Ich mag das Theater nicht.

Page 11

(1) a Ich interessiere **mich** für Theater.

I am interested in theatre.

b **Am** Samstagabend gehe ich oft ins Kino.

On Saturday evening I often go to the cinema.

c Ich **habe** in einer Mannschaft gespielt.

I played in a team.

d Ich spiele einmal **pro** Woche Hockey.

I play hockey once a week.

e Ich **sehe** nicht gern fern.

I don't like (watching) TV.

f Ich turne **seit** drei Jahren.

I've been doing gymnastics for three years.

(2) Ich bin sehr sportlich/ Ich spiele seit fünf Jahren Fußball und trainiere oft/ Ich habe viele Freunde/ Wir gehen am Samstag in die Stadt/ Das Kino ist gut und ich mag das Theater/ Zu Hause gucke ich amerikanische Filme auf meinem Tablet/ Das ist toll!

(3) a Ich spiele gern Tennis.

b Ich treffe meine Freunde.

c Wir gehen ins Kino.

d Meine Schwester sieht gern fern.

e Ich möchte Skateboard fahren.

Page 12

(1) Ad, Ba, Cb, De, Ec

(2) a Ich höre **nicht gern** Musik.

b Ich **sehe** gern Filme auf meinem Laptop.

c Ich sehe **nicht** gern Liebesfilme.

d Ich gehe **am Samstag / samstags** einkaufen.

(3)
a trainieren	train
b Im Großen und Ganzen	overall
c Tablet	tablet
d Blockflöte	recorder
e ab und zu	now and then
f chille	chill (out)

Page 13

(1) a Die Sendung war interessant, **aber** unrealistisch.

The programme was interesting but unrealistic.

b Ich spiele gern Handball **und** fahre gern Ski.

I like playing handball and skiing.

c Wir sitzen um den Weihnachtsbaum **und** öffnen Geschenke.

We sit around the Christmas tree and open presents.

d Kurt hört gern Rapmusik, **aber** er ist noch nie auf ein Konzert gegangen.

My brother likes rap but he has never been to a concert.

(2) a The two topics are unrelated and the tenses are different.

b Not liking opera and having music stored on a tablet are not contrasting ideas.

c The writer's preference for rap is not a reason for the high price of the tickets.

d It's not logical to say they like buying books best if they never go shopping.

(3) 1C, 2A, 3B, 4D

Page 14

1 Tick: b, c, e

2 Illogical order of sentences: The third sentence is about sport so belongs after the first sentence.

Incorrect use of *und* or *aber*: The second sentence should use *und* instead of *aber* because the second part of the sentence is not in contrast to the first part.

Unrelated ideas in the same sentence: None.

Incorrect use of *denn*: In the fourth sentence, *denn* is inappropriate because the second part of the sentence is not a reason for the first part – *und* would be better here.

Missed out a key word: In the fourth sentence, the word *ins* is missing before *Kino*.

Inappropriate use of tense: The fifth sentence should be in the present tense.

Need to start a new sentence: *Das ist nicht köstlich.* can be a separate sentence.

Incorrect adjective used: *köstlich* means 'delicious', not 'costly' or 'expensive'. It would be better to use *teuer* here.

3 Sample answer

Ich bin sportlich. **Ich trainiere einmal pro Woche im Verein.** Ich fahre am Samstag in die Stadt **und** ich treffe Freunde. Ich gehe oft **ins** Kino **und** ich mag das Theater. Zu Hause **sehe** ich gern **fern.** Das ist nicht **teuer!**

Page 15

2 Sample answer

Ich sehe gern fern. Ich gucke Sendungen auf meinem Laptop. Ich höre jeden Tag Musik, aber ich spiele kein Instrument. Ich treffe oft Freunde und wir gehen auf Partys. Sie sind fantastisch. Ich lese ziemlich gern. Ich habe viele Fantasyromane gelesen.

Page 16

Sample answer

Ich gehe oft ins Internet und spiele Computerspiele auf dem Tablet. Ich lese nicht besonders gern, aber ich habe viele Comics gelesen. Ich treffe oft Freunde und wir gehen ins Kino. Ich mag Feste und Feiertage. Ich habe am 31. Dezember Silvester gefeiert.

Unit 3

Page 18

1 Tick: a, b, e

2 **a** i lange, schwarze, hübsch

ii freundlich, sympathisch, (nicht) sportlich

iii gut, lustig

iv nicht so gut

b meine best**e** Freund**in**; **sie**...

3 **a** Meine beste Freundin

b mit meinem Vater

c mit meiner Mutter

Page 19

1 **a** Ich habe einen Bruder. accusative masculine

b Wir wohnen bei unserem Stiefvater. dative masculine

c Meine Freunde sind sehr nett. nominative plural

d Ich verstehe mich gut mit meiner Mutter. dative feminine

2 **a** Mein bester Freund **heißt** Niko.

b Meine beste Freundin **hat** kurze Haare.

c Mein Bruder und ich **verbringen** unsere Freizeit in der Stadt.

d Ich verstehe mich gut mit **meiner** Oma.

e **Mein** Opa hat viel Geduld.

f Ich liebe **meine** Großeltern.

3 **a** **Meine** beste Freundin heißt Sara.

Freundin is feminine and in the nominative case.

b Sara **hat** schwarze Haare.

Need the *er/sie/es* form of *haben*.

c Ich gehe mit **meinem** Freund in die Stadt.

Mit requires the dative, and the ending before a masculine noun is *-em*.

Page 20

1 **a** Bastian und ich **sind** gute Freunde.

Bastian and I are good friends

b Im Sommer **spielen** wir Tennis.

In summer we play tennis.

c Ich kann mit Paula über alles **reden.**

I can talk with/to Paula about everything.

d Ich mag Lotte, weil sie lustig **ist.**

I like Lotte because she's fun/funny.

e Am Wochenende **darf** ich Computerspiele spielen.

At the weekend I'm allowed to play computer games.

f Meine Mutter war streng, als ich elf Jahre alt **war.**

My mother was strict when I was eleven years old.

2 **a** Tobias **hat** immer Zeit für mich.

Tobias always has time for me.

b Ich kann mit Tobias Fußball **spielen.**

I can play football with Tobias.

c Heute **verstehe** ich mich gut mit meiner Stiefmutter.

Today I get/I'm getting on well with my stepmum.

d Wir **verbringen** viel Zeit zusammen.

We spend a lot of time together.

e Sie war streng, als ich ein Kind **war.**

She was strict when I was a child.

f Ich durfte nicht spät nach Hause **kommen.**

I wasn't allowed to come home late.

Page 21

1 a Ein guter <u>freund</u> darf nie (eifersuchtig) sein. Mein bester Freund hat immer <u>zeit</u> (für) mich. Wir (konnen) (über) alles reden. Ich hatte eine sehr (schone) <u>kindheit</u>. Ich durfte jeden <u>tag</u> in den Park gehen. Heute (eibe) ich Fußball und ich (traineire) oft.

b Freund

eifersüchtig

Zeit

für

können

über

schöne

Kindheit

Tag

liebe

trainiere

2 a Ich <u>vebringe</u> viel Zeit mit meinen Freundinnen und <u>Fruenden</u>. Wir sind sehr <u>active</u>. Wir spielen Tennis und gehen <u>shwimmen</u>. Ich mache auch viel mit meiner <u>Family</u>. Wir gehen einkaufen und <u>farhen</u> ab und zu Rad.

b verbringe, Fr**e**unden, akti**v**, **sch**wimmen, Famili**e**, fah**r**en

Page 22

1 Tick: **a**, **b**, **d**, **e**

2 Fruend – spelling error (ue instead of eu)

shlank – spelling error (missing letter c)

haare — missing capital letter

hat – wrong ending (should be *haben*)

mein – wrong ending (should be *meinem*)

reden – word order error (should be at end of sentence)

uber – spelling error (missing umlaut)

Muter – spelling error (missing letter t)

ist – word order error (should be at end of sentence)

fließig – spelling error (ie instead of ei)

3 Mein bester **Freund** ist intelligent und sehr nett. Er ist **schlank** und hat kurze **Haare** und braune Augen. Wir **haben** die gleichen Interessen. Ich verstehe mich auch gut mit **meinem** Stiefvater. Ich kann mit ihm **über** alles **reden**. Aber meine **Mutter** geht mir auf die Nerven, weil sie immer **fleißig ist**.

Page 23

2 Sample answer

Eine gute Freundin ist lustig und man kann mit ihr über alles reden. Das ist sehr wichtig. Ich verbringe meine Freizeit mit Freunden und wir gehen oft ins Kino. Ich verstehe mich gut mit meiner Schwester, aber mein Bruder geht mir auf die Nerven. Ich mache nicht viel mit meiner Familie, aber ab und zu kochen wir.

Page 24

Sample answer

Mein Bruder Noah ist klein und schlank, aber meine Schwester Emilia ist ziemlich groß. Ich verstehe mich gut

mit meiner Mutter, aber mein Bruder und ich streiten uns oft. Ich habe viele Freundinnen und Freunde. Sie sind lustig und aktiv. Wir treiben Sport und gehen einkaufen.

Unit 4

Page 26

1 a in the town centre

b (small) kitchen, (large) living room

c three

d watched TV, read a magazine, played table tennis

e play football (in the garden), go shopping

f nearby

2

		Present	Past	Future
a	Ich wohne mit meiner Familie in einem Haus …	⊘		
b	Im ersten Stock gibt es drei Schlafzimmer.	⊘		
c	Letztes Wochenende war ich am Samstag zu Hause.		⊘	
d	Ich habe ferngesehen …		⊘	
e	… wir haben Tischtennis gespielt.		⊘	
f	… wir werden auch einkaufen gehen.			⊘
g	Die Geschäfte sind in der Nähe.	⊘		

3 **a**, **b**

The following verbs should be circled and annotated as follows:

war	imperfect
habe … ferngesehen	perfect
(habe …) gelesen	perfect
sind … gekommen	perfect
haben … gespielt	perfect
hat … gemacht	perfect

Page 27

1 **a**, **b**

Tick: was du gestern (gegessen hast), was du letztes Wochenende (gemacht hast), was du nicht machen (durftest), als du jünger (warst)

2 **Ad, Bc, Cb, Da**

Tick: D

3 • was du <u>gestern</u> gegessen hast

• was du <u>letztes Wochenende</u> gemacht hast

• was du nicht machen durftest, <u>als du jünger warst</u>

4 Sample answers

a Letztes Wochenende habe ich gefaulenzt.

b Letzte Woche habe ich ein Buch gelesen.

c Am Nachmittag sind wir Rad gefahren.

d Am Samstag bin ich zu Hause geblieben.

Page 28

1
- **a** Meine Schwester hat ferngesehen.
- **b** Mein Bruder hat ein Buch gelesen.
- **c** Sila und Gregor haben Apfelsaft getrunken.
- **d** Wir haben laute Musik gespielt.
- **e** Du hast eine E-Mail geschrieben.
- **f** Der Hund ist in die Küche gegangen.

2
- **Ac** The music was loud.
- **Bd** The news was interesting.
- **Ca** My bedroom was very small.
- **Db** The parents were strict.

3 Um ein Uhr (a) **haben** wir zu Mittag (b) **gegessen**. Fisch und Schnitzel (c) **waren** auf der Karte. Ich (d) **habe** Milch (e) **getrunken**. Das Mittagessen (f) **hat** wunderbar (g) **geschmeckt**. Der Fisch (h) **war** besonders köstlich. Nach dem Essen (i) **sind** wir ins Wohnzimmer (j) **gegangen**. Ich (k) **durfte** keine Computerspiele (l) **spielen**.

Page 29

1
- **a** i S, ii PP, iii H, iv H, v PP, vi H, vii S
- **b** i **bin** ii **gezeigt** iii **haben** iv **habe** v **gegessen** vi **hat** vii **sind**

  war

2 Am Samstag (waren) ich zu Hause mit meiner Austauschpartnerin, Zehra. Wir haben Tischtennis

gespielt   hat

(gespielen). Das (ist) Spaß gemacht. Danach habe ich ein

hat

Buch gelesen und Zehra (hast) Musik gehört. Wir haben

gegessen   gab

dann zu Mittag (essen). Es (gibt) Wurst mit Kartoffeln

hat

und Gemüse. Das (haben) sehr gut geschmeckt.

Page 30

1 An einem Schultag stehe ich um halb acht auf. Ich frühstücke in der Küche und dann gehe ich zur Schule. Am Abend mache ich immer meine Hausaufgaben. Dann bin ich müde und ich sehe gern fern, aber gestern (hatte) ich keine Hausaufgaben und ich (habe) am Computer (gespielt). Gestern Abend habe ich Currywurst (gegessen). Sie (hat) lecker (geschmeckt), weil sie würzig (war). Ich (habe) kein Gemüse (gegessen), denn ich mag das nicht. Nächstes Wochenende werde ich Musik auf meinem Tablet hören und einen Film sehen. Ich werde vielleicht mit meinem Bruder Gitarre spielen.

hatte	had
habe ... gespielt	played
habe ... gegessen	ate
hat ... geschmeckt	tasted
war	was
habe kein Gemüse gegessen	didn't eat

2
- **a** What she drank yesterday
- **b** Ich habe (ein Glas Wasser) getrunken.

Page 31

2 Sample answer

Ich finde das Internet fantastisch. Es hilft bei den Hausaufgaben und ich amüsiere mich mit Computerspielen. Ich habe einen PC, ein Tablet und ein Handy. Letzte Woche habe ich mein Handy jeden Tag benutzt. Ich habe viele Fotos gemacht und mit meinen Freundinnen und Freunden gesimst, aber ich habe nicht telefoniert. Ich finde soziale Netzwerke gut, weil man mit Leuten in Kontakt bleibt. Aber ein Nachteil ist, dass das persönliche Leben nicht privat bleibt. Nächste Woche werde ich mit meinen Freunden simsen, weil es praktisch ist. Aber wir werden auch Tennis spielen – ohne Technologie.

Page 32

Sample answer

Für meine Fitness gehe ich joggen und schwimmen, aber mein Lieblingssport ist Judo. Ich trainiere dreimal pro Woche nach der Schule und das macht Spaß. Ich esse sehr gesund: viel Obst, Gemüse und Milchprodukte. Orangen und Bananen schmecken mir gut. Aber ich trinke zu viel Limonade. Sie ist lecker, aber ungesund. Letzte Woche bin ich im Park joggen gegangen und ich habe auch zweimal Fußball gespielt. Am Donnerstagabend habe ich einen Judowettbewerb gewonnen. Das war sehr gut! Nächste Woche werde ich dreimal schwimmen gehen und vielleicht Taekwondo ausprobieren.

Unit 5
Page 34

1
- **a** Tick: cost of travel, hotel Wi-Fi, seeing the sights
- **b** - travelling by train was very expensive
  - practical because she has her tablet
  - saw many sights yesterday

2

		Present	Past	Future
a	Ich bin ... in London.	✓		
b	Wir sind mit dem Zug gefahren.		✓	
c	Wir übernachten in einem Hotel ...	✓		
d	Gestern haben wir viele Sehenswürdigkeiten gesehen ...		✓	
e	Ich habe ein Geschenk ... gekauft.		✓	
f	... ich möchte Souvenirs kaufen.			✓
g	Das wird interessant sein.			✓

3 **a**, **b**

(morgen) gehen wir – (tomorrow) we are going

möchte … kaufen – would like to buy

werden … gehen – will go

wird … sein – will be

Page 35

1 Tick: wo du übernachten wirst, was du nächste Woche machst, wohin du morgen gehst, deine Pläne für das Wochenende

2 **a**, **b**

	Always refers to the future	May refer to the future	Never refers to the future	English meaning
am Wochenende		✓		at the weekend
nächsten Dienstag	✓			next Tuesday
gestern			✓	yesterday
wenn ich älter bin	✓			when I'm older
morgen früh	✓			tomorrow morning
um 5 Uhr 30		✓		at 5.30

Page 36

1 **a** Ich werde schwimmen gehen.

b Wir werden ins Restaurant gehen.

c Miriam wird Tischtennis spielen.

d Meine Eltern werden um 13 Uhr ankommen.

e Ich werde das Museum besuchen.

f Das wird interessant sein.

2 **a** i Morgen mache ich eine Stadtrundfahrt.

ii Ich werde Souvenirs kaufen.

iii Wir möchten Geschenke suchen.

iv Heute Abend essen wir im Restaurant.

v Meine Schwester will schwimmen gehen.

b i Tomorrow I'm going on a tour of the city.

ii I will buy souvenirs.

iii We'd like to look for presents.

iv Tonight we're eating in a restaurant.

v My sister wants to go swimming.

Page 37

1 **a** Circle: i fliegen ii übernachten iii wird iv wohnen v essen vi gehe

b Underline: i werde iii sein iv möchte v will vi schwimmen

2 **a** ~~werde~~ werden

b ~~schmeckt~~ schmecken

c ~~kaufe~~ kaufen

d ~~werden~~ wird

---

e ~~übernachte~~ übernachten

f ~~fahre~~ fahren

fahren
3 Am Samstag <u>fahre</u> wir nach Stuttgart. Ich möchte

gehen
in der Stadtmitte einkaufen <u>gehe</u> und mein Bruder

besuchen   werden
will ein Museum <u>besucht</u>. Wir <u>werde</u> in einem Hotel

sein
übernachten. Das wird teuer <u>sind</u>. Am Sonntag

möchte   essen
<u>möchten</u> ich schwimmen gehen. Vielleicht <u>esse</u> wir am

Sonntagabend in einem schönen Restaurant.

Page 38

1 **a** Circle: gehen, werde … essen

Translations: are going, will eat

b Underline: Morgen

2 **a** was du heute Abend machen möchtest und warum.

b Student's own answer

Page 39

2 Sample answer

Ich bin mit meiner Familie in Hamburg. Wir sind von London geflogen. Der Flug war schnell, aber nicht bequem. Ich mag Hamburg, weil es viel zu tun gibt und ich kann Deutsch sprechen. Wir werden am Donnerstag eine Stadtrundfahrt machen. Ich möchte den Hafen sehen und vielleicht auch eine Bootsfahrt machen. Gestern Abend sind wir ins Kino gegangen. Dann haben wir in einem schönen Restaurant in der Hafencity gegessen. Der Fisch hat sehr gut geschmeckt. Morgen möchte ich die Geschäfte besuchen und Souvenirs kaufen. Das wird teuer sein. Aber ich empfehle Hamburg!

Page 40

Sample answer

Ich bin mit meiner Familie in Paris. Wir übernachten in einem großen Hotel in der Stadtmitte, in der Nähe vom Eiffelturm. Mein Zimmer ist bequem, aber es gibt viel Lärm. Wir essen jeden Tag im Hotel, weil es praktisch ist. Heute Abend esse ich ein Steak mit Bratkartoffeln. Ich werde Cola trinken. Ich habe schon viele Sehenswürdigkeiten in der Stadt gesehen, zum Beispiel das Musée d'Orsay und die Kathedrale Notre-Dame. Ich habe ein T-Shirt gekauft. Heute Abend machen wir eine Bootstour, weil das Wetter schön ist. Wir werden viel sehen.

Unit 6

Page 42

1 **a** Tick: reason for liking home town, a future stadium, reason for wanting to live in Exeter

b i, v, vi, viii

② and ③ a

Ich wohne in einer kleinen Stadt in Südwestengland. Ich mag meine Stadt, weil es viel zu tun gibt. Wir haben ein Kino, ein Schwimmbad und einen Park. Es wird ein Fußballstadion geben.
Aber in meiner Stadt gibt es auch viel Verkehr und viel Lärm. Das ist ein großer Nachteil.
Letzten Samstag bin ich mit meinem Bruder in die Stadtmitte gegangen. Ich habe Kleidung gekauft und wir haben in einem China-Restaurant gegessen. Mein Bruder hat nichts gekauft.
Ich möchte später in Exeter wohnen, denn es gibt dort eine gute Universität. Ich will nicht auf dem Land wohnen.

Page 43

① Sample answers

a Meine Stadt hat eine **Kirche** und einen **Marktplatz**.

b Ich **mag** die Geschäfte und Restaurants.

c Es gibt kein **Kino** in meiner Stadt.

d Die Sehenswürdigkeiten sind **schön**.

e Ich **gehe zu Fuß** in die Stadt, weil es keine Busse gibt.

f Man sollte die **öffentlichen Verkehrsmittel** verbessern.

g Letzte Woche habe ich **Basketball** im Sportzentrum **gespielt**.

h Ich bin auch ins **Kino** gegangen.

② Ac, Ba, Ce, Dd, Eb

Page 44

① New paragraphs could begin before the response to each bullet point:

Ich wohne in einer kleinen Stadt in Südwestengland. Ich mag meine Stadt, weil es viel zu tun gibt. Wir haben ein Kino, ein Schwimmbad und einen Park. Es wird ein Fußballstadion geben. ‖ Aber in meiner Stadt gibt es auch viel Verkehr und viel Lärm. Das ist ein großer Nachteil. ‖ Letzten Samstag bin ich mit meinem Bruder in die Stadtmitte gegangen. Ich habe Kleidung gekauft und wir haben in einem China-Restaurant gegessen. Mein Bruder hat nichts gekauft. ‖ Ich möchte später in Exeter wohnen, denn es gibt dort eine gute Universität. Ich will nicht auf dem Land wohnen.

② Tick: a, c, e

③ Ae, Ba, Cc, Db, Ed

④ Sample answers

a Es gibt viel für Jugendliche zu tun.

b Wir fahren immer mit dem Auto.

c Das Essen ist lecker.

d Es wird nicht viel Lärm geben.

Page 45

① a denn b und c aber d weil e dann

② a und b aber c also d weil e denn

③ Sample answer

Ich wohne auf einem Bauernhof. Es ist total ruhig, <u>denn</u> es gibt keine Buslinie bis in die Stadt. <u>Also sollte man</u>

die öffentlichen Verkehrsmittel verbessern. Früher habe ich in einer großen Stadt gewohnt. Das war gut, <u>weil es</u> viele Geschäfte und Cafés in der Nähe <u>gab</u>. <u>Aber</u> es gab zu viel Verkehr <u>und</u> das war ein großer Nachteil für mich. In Zukunft möchte ich auf dem Land wohnen. <u>Dann kann ich</u> mit meinem Hund spazieren gehen. <u>Aber</u> meine Schwester will in der Hauptstadt wohnen, <u>denn</u> es ist dort nie langweilig.

Page 46

① and ② a

New paragraphs could begin before the answer to bullet points 3 and 4. It would also make sense to begin a new paragraph before talking about plans for tomorrow:

Ich mache mit meiner Familie Urlaub im Schwarzwald. Die Sonne scheint jeden Tag, aber es ist ziemlich kalt. Gestern hat es geschneit! ‖ Ich bin gern hier, weil ich sportlich bin und es Tennisplätze auf dem Campingplatz gibt. Man kann auch Fahrräder mieten. Es gibt eine Buslinie, also brauchen wir kein Auto. ‖ Morgen fahren wir nach Freiburg und gehen einkaufen. Dann wollen wir ein Picknick machen und vielleicht ein Museum besuchen. ‖ Ich mag den Schwarzwald, aber nächstes Jahr möchte ich lieber in Spanien Urlaub machen, weil das Wetter dort wärmer ist.

② b aber - but it's rather cold

weil - because I'm sporty

und - and there are tennis courts

auch - you can also hire bikes

also - therefore/so we don't need a car

und - and (we're) going shopping

dann - then we want to have a picnic

und - and perhaps visit a museum

aber - but next year I'd rather go on holiday to Spain

weil - because the weather there is warmer

③ a was du dort gemacht hast

b Sample answer

Ich habe gestern Tennis gespielt. Das hat Spaß gemacht.

Page 47

② Sample answer

Ich wohne in Leicester. Ich mag meine Stadt nicht, weil es viel Verkehr gibt. Es sollte mehr Fahrradwege geben. Aber die Geschäfte sind gut und die Stadt hat auch viele Sportplätze.

Nächste Woche werde ich zweimal in die Stadtmitte gehen. Am Mittwochabend gehe ich ins Kino und am Samstag will ich Geschenke kaufen, weil meine Mutter Geburtstag hat.

Letztes Jahr habe ich Köln besucht. Das Wetter war schön, also sind wir jeden Tag spazieren gegangen. Der Dom war interessant, aber es gab viele Touristen.

Meine ideale Stadt ist groß mit modernen Sportanlagen und anderen Aktivitäten für Jugendliche.

Page 48

Sample answer

Wir sind im Urlaub in Cornwall. Das Wetter ist ziemlich warm, also gehen wir jeden Tag an den Strand. Ich liege auch gern in der Sonne und meine Eltern lesen viel.

Wir sind mit dem Auto nach Cornwall gekommen, weil es praktisch und einfach ist. Aber morgen fahren wir mit dem Zug nach St Ives. Das ist eine kleine Stadt an der Küste. Am Donnerstag wollen wir Fahrräder mieten.

Cornwall hat viele Vorteile, aber ich möchte nicht hier wohnen, weil es zu ruhig ist. Meine Stadt ist besser, denn sie hat Sportanlagen, Kinos und viele Geschäfte.

Unit 7

Page 50

① a Tick: preferred career, personal qualities, reason for wanting to work in Switzerland

b Tick: Ich bin geduldig, Die Arbeitszeiten werden oft lang sein, Ich habe Arbeitserfahrung, Ich möchte im Ausland arbeiten

② a Sample answers

i weil ich geduldig bin und ich Menschen helfen möchte.

ii Das wird nie langweilig sein.

iii Das war interessant.

iv Das hat mir keinen Spaß gemacht.

b i present

ii future

iii past

iv past

Page 51

① a interessant
b schwierig
c schrecklich
d teuer
e unterhaltsam
f kreativ
g wichtig
h sympathisch

② a modern
b köstlich
c praktisch
d ekelhaft
e preiswert
f umweltfreundlich

③ Sample answers

a bequem

The rooms in our hotel were comfortable.

b aufregend

I'll go on the roller coaster as I always find it exciting.

c wichtig

We're learning German and Spanish because we think (foreign) languages are important.

d großzügig

I'd like to become an electrician because the pay is generous.

④ a leckeres
b schwierige
c begabte
d unterhaltsame
e tollen
f bequemes

Page 52

① Tick: a, d, f

② Ab, Be, Ca, Dh, Ed, Fg, Gf, Hc

Page 53

① a Kunst ist mein Lieblingsfach, denn die Hausaufgaben **sind** interessant.

b Ich mag Mathe nicht, weil ich schlechte Noten **bekomme**.

c Der Film war nicht gut, weil die Schauspieler unrealistisch **waren**.

d Mein Lieblingssport ist Skifahren, denn ich **bin** gern in den Bergen.

e Ich empfehle das Festival, weil die Musik immer lebhaft **ist**.

② a gibt
b ist
c sind
d will
e bin

③ Sample answers

a ... weil ich aktuelle Themen (nicht) interessant finde.

b ... denn ich mag Tiere (nicht).

c ... weil ich Menschen (nicht) gern helfe.

d ... denn ich bin (nicht) sportlich.

e ... weil ich mich (nicht) für das Theater interessiere.

④ Sample answers

Ich möchte Architekt(in) werden, weil ich Kunst und Mathe mag.

Ich möchte Mechaniker(in) werden, weil ich mich für Autos interessiere.

Ich möchte nicht Feuerwehrmann/-frau werden, weil es sehr anstrengend ist.

Page 54

① Ich bin sehr fleißig in der Schule und bekomme gute Noten. Ich bin pünktlich und zuverlässig. Seit zwei Jahren bin ich Mitglied im Schulorchester. Ich mache das gern, weil ich musikalisch bin. ‖ Ich habe schon in einer Bibliothek gearbeitet. Das war gut, denn ich liebe Bücher. ‖ Ich möchte dieses Jahr in Deutschland arbeiten. Das wird interessant sein, weil ich Französisch und Deutsch lerne und ich meine Sprachkenntnisse verbessern will. Vielleicht kann ich einen Job in einem Hotel bekommen. ‖ Wenn ich älter bin, möchte ich bei einer internationalen Firma arbeiten.

②

Opinion	Reason
likes school orchestra	is musical
liked working in library	loves books
working in Germany will be interesting	learning French and German and wants to improve knowledge of languages

Page 55

2 Sample answer

Ich habe schon viel Arbeitserfahrung. Ich arbeite jeden Samstag in einem Laden in der Stadtmitte und letztes Jahr habe ich mit meiner Mutter in einem Büro gearbeitet. Das war gut, weil ich Geld bekommen habe. Ich habe auch gern mit den Kunden gesprochen. Aber die Arbeitszeiten waren lang. Mein Traumjob? Ich möchte in Zukunft Tierarzt werden, weil ich alle Tiere mag und ich mich für Biologie interessiere. Aber das ist nicht einfach und ich muss sehr gute Noten bekommen. Als Kind wollte ich Lokomotivführer werden, aber jetzt finde ich das uninteressant.

Page 56

Sample answer

Ich interessiere mich für Fremdsprachen. Ich lerne seit fünf Jahren Deutsch und spreche auch Französisch. Ich habe meine Sprachkenntnisse letztes Jahr benutzt. In den Osterferien war ich mit meiner Familie in der Schweiz. Das war gut, weil ich Deutsch und Französisch gesprochen habe. In den Sommerferien bin ich nach Berlin gefahren. Dieses Jahr möchte ich in den Ferien in Österreich arbeiten. Ich mag die Berge und gehe gern wandern. Wenn ich älter bin, möchte ich Touristenführerin werden, denn ich finde Geschichte interessant und ich komme gut mit anderen Menschen aus.

Unit 8

Page 58

1
a favourite subject – *Lieblingsfach*

   or: school trip – *Klassenfahrt*

b habe ... gemacht

c keine

d ich freue mich (auf)

e dürfen + essen

f (in) den Klassenzimmern

g weil es einfach ist

2
a *Schule* is feminine

b it comes after the noun

c *Lieblingsfach* is neuter not feminine

d Although *Biologie* is feminine, it is the subject that is referred to and *das Schulfach* is neuter

e reflexive – ich freue **mich**

Page 59

1 Ac, Bb, Ca, Dd

2
a Jeden Tag sehe ich die Nachrichten.

b Ich treffe gern Freunde.

c Wir lesen Liebesgeschichten.

d Ich mag Zeichentrickfilme, weil sie unterhaltsam sind.

3
a Use the adverb *gern* for 'like' + the present tense (as German does not use the 'ing' form).

b Use the perfect tense: two words, one goes to end of the sentence.

c word order – The verb comes after *zu Hause* ('at home') so it is the second idea in the sentence.

d If using *weil*, the verb goes to the end of the sentence.

4
a Wir spielen gern Handball.

b Ich bin auf ein Festival gegangen.

c Zu Hause sehe ich Videos.

d Ich kaufe Zeitschriften, weil sie interessant sind.

Page 60

1 **a** ⊗, **b** ✓, **c** ✓, **d** ⊗, **e** ⊗, **f** ✓

2
a Finya geht mir auf die Nerven.

b Sie geht mit meinem Bruder aus.

c Wir haben in München Spaß gehabt.

d Ich werde mich besser mit ihr verstehen.

3
a Er versteht sich **ziemlich** gut mit seinem Vater.

b Ich verbringe **zu viel** Zeit vor dem Fernseher.

c Ein guter Freund **muss** viel Geduld **haben**.

d Ihr **Lieblings**hobby ist Schwimmen.

e Paula hat einen **neuen** Freund und er heißt Max.

f Im Moment darf er nicht **aus**gehen.

Page 61

1
a Informatik – ICT

b das Handy – mobile phone

c wandern – to hike

d sympathisch – nice

e nervig – annoying

f das Kind – child

g der Flur – hall, corridor

h das Mobbing – bullying

i der See – lake

j aktuell – current (up to date)

2
a Das war wirklich nervig.

b Ich bin kein Kind.

c Ein Handy ist wichtig.

d Mobbing ist ein Problem.

e Der See war groß.

f Am Dienstag haben wir Informatik.

g Mein Stiefvater ist sympathisch.

h Das ist nicht aktuell.

i Die Katze sitzt im Flur.

j Wir wandern gern.

(3) a nett   e werden

     b dieses Mal   f kommen

     c gedauert   g leiden

     d Zimmer

Page 62

(1) Am Abend wir essen nicht viel. – Verb should be second idea.

Mein Platz ist im ersten Stock. – The correct word for (bed)room is *Zimmer*.

Ich mag meine Wohnung, weil sie ist modern. – Verb after *weil* should go to the end of the clause.

Ich spiele Tennis am Wochenende. – The word *oft* has been omitted.

Meine Schwester findet soziale Netzwerke wichtig. – The sentence has been paraphrased, not translated ('uses' mistranslated as *findet wichtig* (which means 'finds important').

(2) Am Abend **essen** wir nicht viel.

Mein **Zimmer** ist im ersten Stock.

Ich mag meine Wohnung, weil sie modern **ist**.

Ich spiele **oft** Tennis am Wochenende.

Meine Schwester **nutzt** soziale Netzwerke.

(3) a Am Nachmittag treiben / machen wir Sport.

     b Dieses Jahr werde ich viel trainieren.

     c Ich werde oft müde.

     d Mein Lieblingssport ist Leichtathletik, weil er gesund ist.

     e Ich höre Musik, wenn ich zu Hause bin.

     f Wir verbringen sechs Stunden pro Tag in der Schule.

     g Letztes Jahr hatte ich ein Problem mit Mobbing.

Page 63

(1) Sample answers

Bullet point	Difficulty 1	Difficulty 2
I go by bus because it is practical.	'go' – *fahren* not *gehen*	*weil* sends the verb to the end
Trains are a lot more environmentally friendly than cars.	don't leave out 'a lot'	'more environmentally friendly' is all one word in German
Last year we stayed on a campsite.	perfect tense verb consists of two words: one is the second idea and the other goes to the end	which German word to use for 'to stay' – *übernachten* better than *bleiben* here
The soup was nice but the cutlet was cold.	'nice' - *lecker* or *hat gut geschmeckt* (not *nett* or *schön*)	normal word order after *aber*
I am also looking for a present.	'am looking for' is one word, use *suchen* not *sehen* or *gucken*	don't leave out 'also'

(2) Sample answer

Ich fahre mit dem Bus, weil es praktisch ist.

Züge sind viel umweltfreundlicher als Autos.

Letztes Jahr haben wir auf diesem Campingplatz übernachtet.

Die Suppe war lecker, aber das Schnitzel war kalt.

Ich suche auch ein Geschenk.

Page 64

Sample answer

Im Sommer ist es oft zu warm.

Wir verbringen gern viel Zeit mit Freunden.

Letztes Jahr sind sie mit dem Zug gefahren.

Der Campingplatz war ruhig, weil es keine Autos gab.

Ich kann nach Deutschland kommen.

Unit 9

Page 66

(1) a Tick: how often the World Cup takes place, the winner of the 2014 World Cup, watching the World Cup on TV

     b Tick: Die Fußball-Weltmeisterschaft findet alle vier Jahre statt, Meine Freunde interessieren sich für Fußball, Der Flug nach Brasilien ist teuer

(2) a die Weltmeisterschaft

     b im Turnier

     c kämpfen

     d hat stattgefunden

     e in der Schulmannschaft

     f das Finale

     g die Eintrittskarten

     h hat gewonnen

     i Sportarten

     j die Olympischen Winterspiele

Page 67

(1) a teilnehmen   =   mitmachen

     b ich mag Musik   =   ich höre gern Musik   ich bin musikalisch

     c das war toll   =   ich habe das wunderbar gefunden

     d das interessiert mich nicht   =   das ist nichts für mich

     e nicht gut   =   furchtbar   schrecklich

     f billig   =   preiswert   nicht teuer

     g gut   =   super   toll   großartig

(2) Sample answers

     a Die Pariser Modewoche interessiert mich nicht, denn Mode ~~interessiert mich nicht~~ ist nichts für mich.

b Das Festival war gut und ~~die Bands waren gut~~ **ich habe die Bands großartig gefunden**. Die Eintrittskarte war billig. Das Essen war **auch** sehr ~~billig~~ **preiswert** und lecker.

c Ich mag den Eurovision Song Contest, denn ich ~~mag Musik~~ **bin musikalisch**. Mehr also 50 Länder nehmen am Contest teil. In Zukunft will ich auch ~~teilnehmen~~ **mitmachen**.

3 a Mein Bruder hat mit dem Rauchen **angefangen**, weil er etwas Neues **ausprobieren** wollte.

My brother started smoking because he wanted to try something new.

b Drogen sind **gefährlich** und machen **süchtig**.

Drugs are dangerous and addictive.

c Meiner Meinung nach sollte man nicht in der **Öffentlichkeit** vapen, weil es **unsozial** ist.

In my opinion people shouldn't vape in public because it is anti-social.

d Ein Schlafplatz auf der Straße kann **gefährlich** sein.

A place to sleep on the street can be dangerous.

e Ein **Zentrum** für Obdachlose kann bei der Arbeitssuche helfen.

A centre for homeless people can help with looking for work.

f Eine Arbeitsstelle ist wichtig, um eine **eigene** Wohnung zu finden.

A job is important in order to find your own flat.

Page 68

1 a weil **b** als **c** wenn

2 Sample answers

a Wir sparen Energie, wenn wir das Licht ausschalten.

b Ich will eine Fahrradwoche organisieren, weil ich gesund bleiben will.

c Das Projekt hat Spaß gemacht, obwohl es manchmal anstrengend war.

3 Ac, Ba, Cb

4 Sample answers

a Ich möchte meine eigene Wohnung haben.

b Wir wollen unsere Lieblingsmusik hören.

c Man sollte weniger Alkohol trinken.

d Man kann in einem Zentrum für Obdachlose helfen.

e Ich muss eine Arbeitsstelle / einen Job finden.

Page 69

1 Ac, Ba, Cf, De, Ed, Fb

2 a Ich mache eine Umweltaktion **mit** meiner Klasse.

b Meiner Meinung **nach** sollten wir alle den Müll trennen.

c Man könnte öfter **mit** dem Rad fahren.

d Wir interessieren uns sehr **für** den Umweltschutz.

e Viele Tierarten sind **vom** Aussterben bedroht.

f Ich möchte **bei** einer Hilfsorganisation für Straßenkinder arbeiten.

3 a Das Oktoberfest findet jedes Jahr statt.

b Hast du das Festival besucht?

c Das Festival, das ich gesehen habe, war toll.

d Mit vierzehn Jahren hat meine Freundin mit dem Rauchen angefangen.

4 a Das Oktoberfest findet im September statt.

b Meiner Meinung nach ist Alkohol gefährlich.

Page 70

1 Tick: the dangers of smoking, the pros and cons of e-cigarettes, some reasons for drinking alcohol

2 Sample answers

a gefährlich, Öffentlichkeit, süchtig

b Obwohl Rauchen nicht illegal ist, ist es manchmal tödlich.

Wenn man raucht, ist es sehr schwierig aufzugeben.

c Meiner Meinung nach

3 Sample answers

a Viele Menschen trinken Alkohol, um cool zu sein.

b Meine Schwester hat Drogen genommen, als sie jünger war.

c Alkohol kann Spaß machen.

d Ich werde bestimmt nie rauchen.

Page 71

3 Sample answer

In meiner Stadt gibt es zu viele arme Menschen. Arbeitslosigkeit ist hier ein Problem, weil wir keine Industrie mehr haben. Geringe Löhne, Schulden und Bildungsmangel sind auch Probleme und Immigranten sind oft von Armut bedroht. Ich sehe ab und zu Obdachlose in der Stadtmitte. Sie müssen auf der Straße einen Schlafplatz suchen. Ich finde es traurig, dass sie keine eigene Wohnung haben. Sie brauchen Essen und Schutz, weil die Straßen gefährlich sind und weil es im Winter sehr kalt und nass ist. Mein Onkel hatte letztes Jahr Probleme mit Schulden, als er seine Arbeit verloren hat, aber glücklicherweise war er nie obdachlos. Jetzt hat er eine neue Arbeitsstelle gefunden und es geht ihm besser. Es ist nicht einfach, Armen und Obdachlosen zu helfen. Meine Stadt hat ein neues Zentrum, wo Obdachlose essen und duschen können, und das finde ich wichtig. Ich denke, man sollte allen Menschen helfen, Arbeit zu finden.

Page 72

Sample answer

In meiner Schule ist Umweltschutz sehr wichtig. Die Schülerinnen und Schüler interessieren sich für die Umwelt und jedes Jahr gibt es eine Umweltaktion. Dieses Jahr